ENIGMA

Other works by the same author

Roman Converts
John Wesley
The Flight from Reason
Now I See
Within that City
A Saint in the Slave Trade
The Good Gorilla
The Third Day
The Revolt against Reason
Difficulties (*with Mgr. R. A. Knox*)
Is Christianity True? (*with C. E. M. Joad*)
Science and the Supernatural (*with Professor J. B. S. Haldane, F.R.S.*)
Is the Catholic Church Anti-Social? (*with G. G. Coulton*)
Public School Religion. A Symposium
Come What May. An Autobiography
And the Floods Came
Things that have Puzzled Me
Spanish Rehearsal
Communism and Socialism
Whither Europe?
Memory to Memory
A Guide to Montana
Ski-ing
The Alpine Ski Guide to the Bernese Oberland
The Alps
The Englishman in the Alps. An Anthology
Oxford Mountaineering Essays
The Mountains of Youth
Cross Country Ski-ing
Alpine Ski-ing at All Heights and Seasons
A History of Ski-ing
The Story of Ski-ing
Ski-ing for Beginners
Ski-ing in a Fortnight
Mountain Jubilee
Mountains of Memory
Switzerland and the English
Switzerland: Its Literary, Historical and Topographical Landmarks
The Cradle of Switzerland
Zermatt and the Valais
The Italian Lakes
Venice
The Harrovians
Loose Ends
Family Name
Within the Precincts of the Prison
Auction Piquet

ENIGMA

A Study of Moral
Re-Armament

SIR ARNOLD LUNN

LONGMANS, GREEN AND CO
LONDON · NEW YORK · TORONTO

LONGMANS, GREEN AND CO LTD
6 & 7 CLIFFORD STREET LONDON W I
BOSTON HOUSE STRAND STREET CAPE TOWN
605-611 LONSDALE STREET MELBOURNE C I

LONGMANS, GREEN AND CO INC
55 FIFTH AVENUE NEW YORK 3

LONGMANS, GREEN AND CO
20 CRANFIELD ROAD TORONTO 16

ORIENT LONGMANS PRIVATE LTD
CALCUTTA BOMBAY MADRAS
DELHI HYDERABAD DACCA

First published 1957

Printed in Great Britain by
The Camelot Press Ltd., London and Southampton

To LIEUTENANT-COLONEL L. F. SHERIDAN, O.B.E.

My dear Sherry,

On the only occasion I mentioned M.R.A. to you your reaction was one of acute distaste, but you have often registered a mild interest in the peculiar characteristics of religious communions and a certain curiosity as to the degree of influence which they exercise on the secular activities of this distracted planet. And I am therefore sanguine enough to hope that you may not regret the publication of a book which is a sincere attempt to arrive at an unbiased judgement on a movement which is represented in over a hundred countries.

Moreover, you will, I know, agree that one's judgement of the achievements of a religious group must not be unduly influenced by one's distaste for the idiom in which their doctrines are presented. And once this is conceded there is clearly place for an attempt to assess the contribution which M.R.A. is making to peace in industry and to the defence of the free world against Communism.

I summarised the main evidence for M.R.A. achievement in a long appendix which I reluctantly scrapped before sending the MS to the publishers and the typescript had to be cut by a further 15,000 words before publication. But I hope that the book even in its abbreviated form will convince you that M.R.A. has already had a small but definite influence on industrial relations, as for example their success in reconciling management and labour in the National Airlines of America. A feud which lasted years and caused one of the longest strikes in airlines history was 'brought to a screeching halt as the result of Moral Re-Armament', according to W. T. Babbit, vice-president of the Air Line Pilots of America.

Similarly in the struggle against Communism M.R.A. has had some influence not only in Europe, but also in Africa and Asia. In this connection, I refer the reader to one of the most important Catholic tributes to M.R.A. from the Dean of the Faculty of Catholic Theology in Bonn which I have quoted in Appendix II.

A movement like a man may be judged not only by its friends but also by its enemies. M.R.A. has on many occasions been attacked on the Moscow radio, and its bitterest enemies in the Trade Union movement are all those who have a vested interest in aggravating class war.

Neither the presentation of M.R.A. on platforms at Caux nor the idiom of M.R.A. appeals to me but I have been deeply impressed by the quality of life produced by this movement and by the heroic self-sacrifice which it inspires. I do not think that any Christian should be tricked into sneering at any group of men and women who are passionately sincere in their determination both to discover and to implement the will of God.

Be that as it may, M.R.A. is a world movement which can no longer be dismissed by a few snap judgements based on a brief visit to Caux and a casual study of M.R.A. literature. A Catholic would be unimpressed by a railing attack on monasticism by a writer who had only spent three days in a guest house of a monastery, and read half a dozen books on monasticism.

I dedicate this book to you for many reasons. I owe to you some of the most interesting experiences in a long and varied life for it was you who recruited me into an organisation instituted to do harm by stealth and blush to find it in fame, and our friendship which began in the war has been reinforced during the long years of uneasy peace.

Yours ever,
Arnold Lunn.

MÜRREN, 30th JANUARY, 1957.

CONTENTS

ACKNOWLEDGMENTS

WE are indebted to the author's representatives for permission to reproduce extracts from "In Praise of Wine" by Hilaire Belloc, to Messrs. C. A. Watts & Co. Ltd. for material from *Inside Buchmanism* by Geoffrey Williamson, and to Moral Re-Armament for permission to quote from documents in their possession.

I

APPROACH TO THE PROBLEM

I ADJUSTED my belt, and as the plane took off from New York to Zurich I opened a parcel containing Monsignor Ronald Knox's *Enthusiasm* which I read without a break, except for meals, until the small hours of the morning, and this in spite of the interruptions of a young Swiss who was anxious to discover whether I had ever heard of myself. 'I once met at Mürren the English ski-pioneer Arnold Lunn. You will certainly have heard of him?' I admitted that we were, in a manner of speaking connected since Arnold Lunn's wife was the mother of my son. He was so dismayed by this avowal of illicit relations with Arnold Lunn's wife that he did not interrupt me again.

The word 'enthusiasm' is derived from two Greek words, *en* within, *theos* God, and strictly speaking means god-possessed. The enthusiast, as this term was understood by John Wesley's enemies, was a man who appealed against ecclesiastical authority to the god within. 'Sir,' said Bishop Butler to John Wesley, 'the pretending to extraordinary revelations and gifts of the Holy Ghost is a horrid thing—a very horrid thing.' The good Bishop clearly bracketed Methodists with Quakers as theological anarchists for ever appealing against ecclesiastical authority to the 'Inner Light'.

Enthusiasm, in the correct sense of the term, is a phenomenon which recurs again and again in Church history in connection with different sects, such as Montanists, Anabaptists, Quietists, Illuminists and Quakers. Monsignor Knox's book fascinated me because it gave coherence to my own desultory reading over a period of some forty years. Many of the books which he quotes I had read. One of the books which he quotes, *John Wesley*, I had written. I was brought up as an Anglican by my Anglican mother, but my father, the late Sir Henry Lunn, was a

Methodist, and it was he who first awakened my admiration for one of the greatest Englishmen of the eighteenth century, John Wesley.

My only criticism of Monsignor Knox's book is that the urbane objectivity which informs his discussion of the earlier enthusiasts is absent from his occasional contemptuous references to M.R.A. He would seem to have recoiled in shuddering distaste from Dr. Buchman and his followers. It would appear that Monsignor Knox only likes Enthusiasts when they are dead.

M.R.A. repays study not only because it resembles earlier manifestations of Enthusiasm but for its unprecedented attitude to the Catholic Church. Hitherto Enthusiasts have been either hostile to the Church or, in the case of manifestations of this phenomenon within the Church, hostile to ecclesiastical authority. The Enthusiasts of M.R.A. have never made the slightest attempt to discourage, and in some cases have actively encouraged, conversions to the Church, and have been responsible for persuading far more than a hundred lapsed Catholics to return to the practice of their religion.[1]

Whereas Enthusiasts in general appeal to the authority of the Inner Light against ecclesiastical authority, it is a basic principle of M.R.A. that 'Guidance', which partially corresponds to the Quaker's Inner Light, should always be checked and controlled by the teaching of the Church to which the individual belongs.

Even more surprising than the attitude of these Enthusiasts to the Catholic Church is the attitude of the Catholic Church to M.R.A. That the majority of Catholic bishops should discourage Catholics from co-operating with M.R.A. was only to be expected, but what is wholly without precedent is that one Cardinal and more than one Catholic bishop should have encouraged Catholics who were attracted by M.R.A. to pay

---

[1] M.R.A. badly need a good archivist for their records are inadequately kept. It was only comparatively recently that it occurred to them to keep an exact record of former communists who had returned to the full practice of the faith under M.R.A. influence. A list of over a hundred names and addresses of such communists was handed in to the Holy Office at Rome by Count Armande de Malherbe, but this list contains only the names of those who reported their return to the Faith during a comparatively short period.

regular visits to the Swiss headquarters at Caux. I am writing this introductory chapter on 26th June 1956, and it is not impossible that Catholics may be forbidden to take any further part in M.R.A. by the time the book is published. Even so, I have no more reason to regret the time that I have spent on the study of M.R.A. than has Monsignor Knox to deplore the many years of research which he had devoted to their predecessors.

Admittedly it is only a minority who are as interested as Monsignor Knox or William James in *The Varieties of Religious Experience*, the title of James's most famous book, but it is for this minority that Monsignor Knox wrote *Enthusiasm*, and that I am writing *Enigma*, and I am not prepared to admit that it is more important for the minority who are interested in Church history to be informed about manifestations of Enthusiasm, such as the Montanists and Quietists, who have vanished from the world, than about the new Enthusiasts who are influencing the world in which we live.

'The fact is,' as a priest remarked to me at Caux, 'that M.R.A. can no longer be dismissed in a few contemptuous clichés. There is something here which is important, something which we Catholics must try to understand.'

Nobody could look less like the creator of a world-wide movement than Dr. Buchman. What is the secret of his success? Why has France bestowed on him the Legion of Honour, and Germany, Greece and Japan decorations which rank with the Legion of Honour? Why have more than a hundred nations, among them Japan and Burma, Egypt, Nigeria, Persia and Brazil, sent their representatives to Caux? Many of them have been members of parliament, some of cabinet rank. Dr. Adenauer has been to Caux and invited M.R.A. to send a team to Germany. M. Robert Schuman has spoken at Caux Assemblies in terms which entitle M.R.A. to claim him as a supporter. What would be the answer of all those who have come from remote lands to the question with which wartime posters familiarised us—'Is your journey really necessary?'

It was in the hope of finding an answer to these and other questions that I returned again and again to Caux where I have spent an aggregate of just under six months in the last three years, and have also established contact with M.R.A. in London, New York, Washington, Los Angeles, Germany and Italy.

During my first week-end at Caux I was the guest of Mr. Robert Readhead, but on all subsequent visits I paid more than I should have paid elsewhere as I was anxious to be unfettered by any financial obligation to M.R.A.

Terminology

'The success and enduring influence of any systematic construction of truth,' wrote Archbishop Trench in his classic study of words, 'depends as much on an exact terminology as upon close and deep thinking itself. Hardly any original thoughts have assumed their proper importance in the mind of inventors until aptly selected words and phrases have nailed them down and held them fast.'

Unfortunately the apostles of M.R.A. do not share the Archbishop's bias in favour of exact terminology and have felt no obligation to produce a word to describe those who practise the spiritual discipline known as Moral Re-Armament. They have, therefore, only themselves to blame if the world calls them 'Buchmanites' or 'Groupers'. It is, of course, as offensive to write about the Moral Re-armers as 'Buchmanites', as to write about Catholics as 'Papists', or about Muslims as Mohomedans. As 'grouper' is the name of a fish, I am not surprised that the apostles of M.R.A. dislike being described as fish, but their interest in terminology began and ended by raising objections to the terms popularised by those outside the Group, or to my own suggestions such as 'Groupist' or 'Moral Re-armer', for members of the M.R.A. movement.

They are not even prepared to admit that M.R.A. is a movement. 'A movement,' they will tell you, 'is something which you can join or leave. You can't join M.R.A. You can only live it.' I agree that M.R.A. is a spiritual discipline, the essence of which is the Quiet Time, Guidance and Sharing, but it is not *only* a spiritual discipline. A movement is necessary to carry the message of M.R.A. to the world. The hotels at Caux are not the property of a spiritual discipline. The London headquarters in Berkeley Square are not owned by a spiritual discipline. The properties which belong to M.R.A. are in the possession of legally constituted bodies which have been created by a movement.

'That's all very plausible,' an MRA friend of mine replied, 'but once we allow ourselves to be called a movement we shall aggravate the difficulty of persuading the world that we are not a sect, and there is no analogy whatever between Dr. Buchman's position in M.R.A. and Luther's position in Lutheranism.'[1]

Resenting as they do being labelled as 'Buchmanites', it is all the stranger that they should take so little trouble to achieve precision instead of woolliness in their terminology, another symptom, perhaps, of their distrust of philosophy which will be discussed in a later chapter. I became such a bore on this subject that finally Mr. Lionel Jardine in despair suggested: 'An MRA' to describe an individual who follows the Moral Re-armament way of life, the equivalent plural being MRAs. I have adopted this suggestion only because I can think of nothing better.

Zetesis

There is an immense literature on M.R.A. which is in the main the work either of ardent propagandists or of hostile critics. There is no study of M.R.A. written in the idiom of research. The nearest approach to such a work is a little booklet by Maisie Ward. This brief essay is a valuable source for the study of the Oxford Group in its earlier phases, and is in respect of charity a model which I would have done well to

---

[1] An MRA who read the typescript of this book said: 'You don't talk about "The Catholic Movement".' In point of fact I would not in the least object to referring to the 'Catholic movement in the Church of England' and I cannot understand why it should be appropriate to write of 'The Oxford Movement' and not of the 'M.R.A. Movement'. Some such word is needed, as indeed the MRAs themselves recognise, but even Francis Goulding who read the typescript could not agree on *one* word to substitute for 'movement' and in one part of the typescript suggested 'work' and at another 'agency'. I should be interested to discover what word MRAs would substitute for 'movement' in the following sentence, which occurs in the last chapter of this book: 'It is indeed a strange coincidence that the eastern and western ends of the Lake Leman should have provided headquarters for two great religious movements, Calvinism at Geneva and M.R.A. at Caux.'

follow in a chapter of my book, *The Good Gorilla*, which I wrote describing a 'House Party' at Interlaken. Maisie Ward is one of those Catholics who realise, as indeed most intelligent Catholics do realise, that the unique position which we claim for the Church among Christian communions creates corresponding obligations, and that the principle of *noblesse oblige* should influence all that we write and say about Christians who are not of our Communion. It is merely irritating when the old anti-Catholic canards, as, for instance, that Jesuits teach that the end justifies the means, or that mediaeval philosophers spent their time debating how many angels could dance on the point of a needle, appear again and again, even in the writings of men with some pretensions to scholarship, but it is not only irritating but disedifying when Catholics sink to this level in writing about other Christians. Charity does not forbid criticism or even condemnation, but it does forbid ill-informed criticism.

That Mr. Geoffrey Williamson, the special correspondent of *John Bull*, should spend four days at Caux as the guest of M.R.A., and on the strength of this write a book *Inside Buchmanism*, is merely of incidental interest as a revelation of the secular mind. The proper title should, of course, have been *Inside Williamson*, but it is not a precedent which will be followed by any serious students of M.R.A.

'Happy is the man,' said Euripides, 'who understands the value of research.' The trouble with so many of those who have written snappy articles or booklets about M.R.A. is that they have lacked *Zetesis*, which literally means 'searching', but which crystallises in seven letters one of the notes of Hellenism, an eager, restless curiosity, the fruits of which are as valuable in religion as in scientific research. The good controversialist, said Chesterton, must be a good listener. He must be as anxious to extract reliable information about his opponent's position as a spy to discover the plans of an enemy. He must have *Zetesis*. And what is true of the controversialist is no less true of all those who write about religious or political movements with which they themselves are out of sympathy. What they write will be of value in proportion to the time and trouble that they have taken to discover what is the

best possible case that can be made out for the beliefs which
they reject.

No critical study of a Religion or a Church or a Religious
Group is satisfactory unless there is some measure of collabora-
tion between the critic and those he criticises. This col-
laboration may consist of nothing more than a careful study
of all the best that has been written in defence of the doctrines
criticised, or it may be formal and explicit, as in the case of
books consisting of an exchange of letters between men with
sharply opposing views. I have collaborated in four such
books, my sparring partners being Monsignor R. A. Knox
(before I became a Catholic), the late C. E. M. Joad, Professor J. B. S. Haldane, F.R.S., and the late Dr. G. G. Coulton.
I am grateful to the distinguished men who crossed swords
with me, for I acquired from these duels a habit of prudence
in controversy which has stood me in good stead. Rash and
uninformed criticisms of beliefs which one rejects are not particularly intelligent, even if committed to paper in a book of
which one is the sole author, but they are suicidal if one risks
exposure within the covers of a book on the title page of which
one's name appears as part-author.

A similar exchange of controversial letters would be inap-
propriate in the case of the present book, for I am writing not
as a controversialist but as an investigator sincerely anxious
to present an honest and unbiased report, an investigator who
has tried to make his own the guiding principle of that great
Catholic historian, Lingard, 'to observe the events with the
coolness of an unconcerned spectator'. Nonetheless I have
adopted what is in effect the basic principle of all debates,
written or verbal. I have submitted every chapter as it was
written to my friends in M.R.A., and have often modified what
I have written as the result of their criticisms.

Most of my friends in M.R.A. would have preferred me to
write another kind of book, a Catholic variant of Peter
Howard's books, but I know they will agree that those who
write on M.R.A. must practise what M.R.A. preaches—
'Absolute Honesty'. Absolute moral standards are unattainable in this world even by saints, but the degree in which this
book approximates to the ideal of absolute honesty will be

determined by the influence on the author of certain considerations.

It would not, to cite the most important of these considerations, be even relatively honest to censor what I have written in order to please my friends in M.R.A. On the other hand, uninformed candour is often indistinguishable from insincerity, for a man who will not take the trouble to discover whether his 'candid opinion' is just or unjust cannot be credited with that intellectual integrity which is of the essence of sincerity. It is not true that every man 'has a right to his opinion'. No man has a right to believe that twice two is five. We have no right to be wrong. On the contrary we have an obligation to inform ourselves correctly and to avoid talking nonsense. From which it follows that the critic of beliefs which he does not share must make every effort to ascertain the best defence of those beliefs.

Finally, it is not even relatively honest to compare the best in one's own Church with the worst in other communions. Every Church and every religious revival both within and without the Church has its lunatic fringe, for man is corrupted not only by original sin but also by original silliness. Again, it is salutary for Catholics to remember that Chaucer and Chartres and Michelangelo are not the only products of Catholic culture, for the Church in her infinite charity caters not only for those who like the best but also for those who like the worst, the worst not only in ecclesiastical art but also in devotional literature. My brother, who wrote under the name of Hugh Kingsmill, published an anthology, *The Worst of Love*, which consisted of the silliest love poems and love letters in the language. It would be easy to compile a companion anthology, *The Worst of Divine Love*, by a corresponding selection from the more inane forms of devotional literature.

II

THE AESTHETIC CONSCIENCE

Is Nature her own explanation? Is matter the ultimate reality? Is the supernatural a myth? Are there ultimate values which will survive the death of the solar system? Does man survive the grave? No problems which have occupied the mind of man are more important than these, and yet such is the tyranny of irrational fashion that research concerned with these ultimate problems enjoys incomparably less prestige than research which throws light on the physical nature of the universe. When Leverrier discovered the planet Neptune he received the plaudits of the scientific world and was recognised and honoured as a man who had enriched science with an epoch-making discovery, and yet, though the world was a little wiser for his discovery, nobody was the wealthier or the healthier. The practical influence of this discovery on human life was precisely nil.

On the other hand, the demonstration beyond all possible doubt that man survives the grave would have a revolutionary effect on mankind. Yet few forms of research are less fashionable than those which are concerned with evidence which suggests the existence of the supernatural. Sir Oliver Lodge told me that he had lost his chance of the presidency of the Royal Society because of his interest in psychical research. Alexis Carrell, who investigated the miracles at Lourdes and was converted from scepticism by the discovery that miraculous cures were, as he said, 'stubborn irreducible facts, which must be taken into account', tells us that he began the study of miracles at a time when 'it was difficult for a young doctor, and dangerous for his future career, to become interested in such a subject'. What a reflection on the contemporary scientists, for as Carrell justly observed, 'Science has to explore the whole of reality.'

B

Aesthetic Prejudice

T. H. Huxley summed up his conception of his scientific ideal in a famous letter to Charles Kingsley: 'Sit down before fact as a little child, be prepared to give up every preconceived notion, follow humbly wherever and to whatever abysses Nature leads, or you shall learn nothing.'

A fine ideal, which Huxley found it easier to preach than to practise; when he was invited by the Dialectical Society to join the Committee which was investigating the remarkable mediumship of Daniel Douglas Hume, Huxley declined the invitation. 'Supposing the phenomena are genuine, they do not interest me . . .' What a bizarre admission! Thirteen reputable witnesses had stated that they had seen in good light, for Hume always objected to darkness in his seances, 'heavy bodies—in some instances men—rise slowly in the air and remain there for some time without visible support'. If their evidence deserved to be taken seriously, it seemed as if phenomena had been proved to occur which were wholly inconsistent with the scientific outlook of the age, and yet Huxley could assert that such phenomena, revolutionary in their implications, did not interest him.

Huxley continued: 'The only good I can see in the demonstration of the truth of "Spiritualism" is to furnish an additional argument against suicide. Better live a crossing-sweeper than die and be made to talk twaddle by a "medium" hired at a guinea a seance.'

But the question at issue was not whether the life of a crossing-sweeper was richer and more varied than the life of a spirit, but whether certain physical phenomena, revolutionary in their implications, had been observed, and whether the spirit communications had been proved. The spiritualist might have rejoined, 'Sit down before fact like a little child, be prepared to give up every preconceived notion, follow humbly wherever and to whatever abysses Nature leads, even to the abyss of a spiritualist's heaven, or you shall learn nothing.'

Instead, Huxley sat down before unwelcome facts as a little child confronted by something which the child dislikes. Like a bored or irritated child he squirmed and wriggled and averted his gaze. Huxley's scientific conscience was not proof against the grotesque and ludicrous aspects of spiritualism, but the evidence that Hume possessed supernormal powers was so strong that Huxley, had he been true to his scientific code, could not have refused the Dialectical Society's invitation. It was Huxley's aesthetic prejudices which stifled the still, small voice of his scientific conscience.

In a book[1] which I was writing when I first met Dr. Buchman, I drew a parallel between Huxley's refusal to investigate Hume and the prevailing lack of interest in the remarkable claims made by and on behalf of Dr. Buchman so far as the finances of his vast and expensive projects are concerned. If it be true that Dr. Buchman and his colleagues are 'guided' to send big teams to South Africa, India or Canada as the case may be, if the plans are often approved when there is no money to meet the day-to-day expenses, if the full-time workers in this movement draw no salary and act with sunny confidence in the belief that 'where God guides He provides', and if this confidence is always justified and the money, whether for teams or for individuals, is always forthcoming, though often at the very last moment, then we are confronted with facts which it is difficult, if not impossible, to reconcile with an atheistic or materialistic philosophy. Such facts are therefore supremely worth investigating, but the overwhelming majority of those who criticise M.R.A. have no intention of examining them, and this for many reasons of which aesthetic prejudice is not the least important. There is an admirable diagnosis of this prejudice in Harold Begbie's book on the Oxford Group, *Life Changers*.

Among the Life Changers whose reactions to Dr. Buchman are described in this book was an Oxford man of twenty-four who had taken First Class Honours in the Oxford School of Philosophy, colloquially known as 'Greats'. The Oxford Greats man quotes the illuminating remark of a German, ' "You English," said the German, "are always at the mercy of your aesthetic conscience, an instinctive reaction against some forms

---

[1] *The Flight from Reason* (1931), rewritten and republished under the title of *The Revolt Against Reason* (1951).

of behaviour which seem to you out of place, vulgar, theatrical.
This aesthetic conscience is right ninety-nine times out of a
hundred; in the hundredth case it will prevent you from helping or appreciating a man whose constitution or education are
radically different from your own." ' And the Greats man
continues, 'My aesthetic conscience had a hard time of it with
the Americans. I felt myself in an alien culture.' 'I have dwelt
on this first meeting,' he continues, 'rather because of its immediate strangeness than because of its results. For the first
time in my life I had deliberately and gladly made a fool of
myself before a perfect stranger. I had told him things I had
never breathed to another; I had told him of all my laugh-
able vanities and dishonesties that make the stuff of a man's
most intimate life.'

It would be easier to understand Dr. Buchman's influence
over sophisticated Oxonians if he were a second Newman
speaking the same language as his disciples, and a product of
the same tradition. But this is not the case. 'Some of these
men,' writes the Oxford Greats man, 'spoke to me with troubled
criticism of their leader, disliking as I did his theological
opinions, but all sticking to him with an unconquerable loyalty
as the man who had worked a great miracle in their lives, and
who was by far the most remarkable man of their experience.'

Aesthetic Dissuasions

It is difficult to examine dispassionately the reasoned arguments for a Church or, as in the case of M.R.A., for a religious
way of life, if the dissuasions are much stronger than the suasions. Of course, one man's suasions may be another man's
dissuasions. More Protestants are repelled than attracted by
the continuity of the Catholic Church with the Greco-Roman
civilisation which is the foundation of the culture of Christendom. For some this continuity is clear evidence that the
Catholic Church is still partially pagan; for others it is proof
that the Church, precisely because she is divine, can assimilate
and consecrate all that was noblest in paganism. It is, as
Tyrrell somewhere says, a greater triumph to capture an
enemy's fleet than to sink it.

In the Catholic Church there is not only unbroken continuity with pre-Christian Rome and Athens, but also interrupted continuity as, for instance, in the Trochaic metres which vanished from Latin poetry at about the time of Ennius, and reappeared in the hymns of the mediaeval Church; but no such subterranean stream of classical culture surfaces at Caux, and something wider than the Atlantic separates the American founder of the Oxford Group whose spiritual message is conveyed by engineering analogies—'The Electronics of the Spirit'—from the architect of the Oxford Movement.

> Passages, which to a boy, [writes Newman] are but rhetorical commonplaces which he imitates as best he can in his own flowing versification, and thinks neither better nor worse than a hundred others, at length come home to him when he has had experience of life and pierce him with their sad earnestness and vivid exactness. Then he comes to understand how it is that lines, the birth of some chance morning or evening at an Ionian festival or among the Sabine hills, have lasted for generation after generation for thousands of years with a power over the mind and a charm which the current literature of his own day with all its obvious advantages is utterly unable to rival.

There is nothing at Caux which links M.R.A. with our remote parentage, no haunting echoes of lines 'born among the Sabine hills', and there is nothing at Caux which recalls, as even the ugliest of Catholic chapels recalls, the lyrical loveliness of mediaeval art and song. And yet if M.R.A. ever adopts a patron saint I am sure that St. Francis of Assisi will be Dr. Frank Buchman's choice. '*If everybody cared enough, and everybody shared enough, everybody would have enough . . .*' The sentiment is Franciscan even if the idiom be Frank, and those who dislike the idiom should remember that the 'Fioretti of Frank' appeal to many who would be unmoved by the 'Little Flowers of St. Francis'.

Though I prefer the idiom of St. Francis and of Newman to the idiom of M.R.A. I fully realise that the appeal of M.R.A. to Asia and Africa is strengthened rather than weakened by the complete break with the classical tradition. Catholic missionaries in Asia were the first to realise that the Church was handicapped by a presentation too closely identified with

European culture. An idiom which may attract one potential convert repels another, and just as our Lord adapted His message to His audience, for we may be sure that the language in which He conversed with the doctors in the Temple was not the language in which He addressed the simple people, the Catholic Church, while proclaiming in every century and in every continent the same unchanging truths, varies her presentation from age to age and from place to place.

'I hear you're an author,' the Abbot of a Trappist monastery in America remarked to me when he received me. 'I wish you'd write something about us, we could do with a little publicity.' A European Abbot who was anxious to increase Trappist vocations might have encouraged an author to make the nature of this vocation better known, but he would have translated his wishes into a different idiom.

The same unchanging truths can be conveyed not only in different languages but in different dialects of the same language. As indeed I discovered during the months that I was attached to the Faculty of the Catholic University of Notre Dame, Indiana, best known to Protestants for its football teams. Here are some extracts from the Religious Bulletin distributed daily to the undergraduates.

In a Body for the Team

Phil Bondi, President of the S.A.C., has asked that a public student Mass be offered in the main church every Saturday morning for the protection of the team. Certain students will help you get up. When you hear their voices turn out! Come to the church and offer your Masses and Holy Communions together with the Celebrant. Nearly all members of the football squad will be with you at the Communion rail—or they will be very different from the great Notre Dame teams of the past.

And here is the announcement of a Special Mission to Students, addressed to a hypothetical undergraduate who is about to call up his girl on the telephone.

Upper class man! Call up Tiddybelle and say to her: 'This coming week, my Precious Sparkler, I shall be busy, pre-occupied, heavily engaged. My soul is in for its annual renovation. After a year or so, even the best kind of guy needs some renovation.'

Many undergraduates with literary ambitions poked fun at these Religious Bulletins. The idiom in which they were written appealed to them as little as the idiom of M.R.A. appeals to me. But they were effective with those for whom they were intended.

The criterion of religious literature is motive and effectiveness. Nobody who was in touch with the Editor of the Bulletin could doubt that his life was dedicated to one supreme purpose, fortifying the undergraduates against the temptations and infidelities of an increasingly secular civilisation, and no Christian who had visited Caux could deny that the overriding motive of every MRA is the determination to transform our corrupted civilisation through lives dedicated to the unquestioning service of God.

III

BACKGROUND TO CAUX

IT was in July 1930, at Mürren, that I first met Dr.
Buchman. He was attending a Reunion Conference convened by my father, the late Sir Henry Lunn. It was in
1892 that my father first invited leading ecclesiastics to discuss the problem of a divided Christendom, and as the years
passed he began, as I know, to wonder whether any practical
results had been achieved. These conferences may well have
strengthened natural alliances, as for instance between Low
Churchmen and Nonconformists, but they did nothing to
bridge the gap between Anglo-Catholics and all who rejoiced
to describe themselves as Protestants. The same old chips remained on the same old shoulders.

It was my memory of these conferences which enabled me
to appreciate the amazing co-operation of men of different
faiths at Caux.

Dr. Buchman was quiet and detached. Many years later I
asked him for his impression of the Mürren Conference. 'I listened to many speeches,' he replied with a chuckle, 'and I
don't remember a word that anybody said, and what's more
I don't think any of the speakers remember what they said.'

One's memory of the past is always coloured by contemporary
impressions, and it may therefore be useful to record what I
wrote within a short time of meeting Dr. Buchman.

I asked him how he financed the sending of missionary groups
during the Long Vacation from Oxford to South Africa. 'I never
ask for money,' he replied, 'either in print or in any other way.
I do not bother about finance, but as you ask a definite question, I will try to answer it. The money we need turns up somehow. For instance, we had booked our passages to South Africa,
but there was no money to pay for our passages until twenty-four
hours before the ship sailed, and then it came as a spontaneous
gift.'

And as I was in the transition stage from agnosticism to Catholicism I added, 'He gave me other odd instances of what he chose to describe as "answers to prayer".' Five years later I recalled our meeting.

> The most impressing thing about Buchman is that he is not impressive. Neither his appearance nor his manner provide any clue to the solution of a puzzling problem, the problem of the origin and growth of this remarkable movement. . . . I liked Buchman's habit of wandering off into the mountains for his 'Quiet Times'. . . . I was attracted rather than repelled by this un-English, un-Oxford, unacademic American evangelist. None the less I resisted firmly his invitation to pray with him and to join one of his house parties at Oxford. . . .[1]

Dr Frank Buchman and the Start of His Work

Frank Nathan Daniel Buchman was born at Pennsburg, Pennsylvania, on 4th June 1878. His family came first to Pennsylvania from St. Gallen, Switzerland, in the year 1740. Dr. Buchman graduated from Muhlenberg College in 1899. He was ordained as a Lutheran Minister in 1902.

From 1902 to 1907 Dr. Buchman was in charge of a hospice for the underprivileged of Philadelphia. The committee who controlled the hospice asked him to reduce the rations of the young people who were in his charge. Dr. Buchman objected to the order and resigned.

Dr. Buchman's health had been affected by overwork, so he went abroad and found himself in the summer of 1906 in Keswick. In a country chapel near Keswick he heard a woman speak of the Cross of Christ, and 'suddenly had a poignant vision of the Crucified'.

> 'That same day,' he writes, 'God used me to change the life of a Cambridge student who was at this time studying at Keswick. I saw that when I obeyed God, miracles happened. I learnt the truth that when man listens, God speaks; when man obeys, God acts; when men change, nations change.'

He wrote to the six committee men in Philadelphia asking

[1] *Within That City* (1936), pp. 158-78.

their forgiveness for the ill-will which he had harboured against them, and to these letters he received no reply.

From 1909 to 1915 he was at the State College, Pennsylvania, and it is claimed that when he left 1,200 students out of 1,600 were attending Bible classes. His work in bringing back some lapsed Catholics to the practice of their religion was publicly acknowledged by the Catholic Chaplain.

From 1916 to 1921, Dr. Buchman held an extension lectureship under the Hartford Theological Foundation, and between 1915 and 1919 engaged in religious activities for extensive periods in India, Korea, Japan, China and the Philippines.

From 1921 to 1922 Dr. Buchman was a member of Westminster College, Cambridge (the college for Presbyterian postgraduate courses), and attended lectures. In May 1921 Dr. Buchman visited Oxford, and it was in A. S. Loudon Hamilton's rooms in Christ Church that the Oxford Group came into being. I met Loudon Hamilton many times at Caux, and it would be difficult to conceive of anybody less likely to be attracted by a wandering American evangelist. His background, to use the current argot, was definitely 'U', the right kind of family, the right kind of school, a distinguished career in the war in the course of which he won an M.C. for gallantry, and then Christ Church, Oxford.

Loudon Hamilton not only told me the story of his conversion but was kind enough to put what he had said into writing, and it is from this record that I am quoting.

Loudon Hamilton's Story

It was in Christ Church in May 1921 that a friend of mine asked me casually if I would like to meet an American Professor visiting Oxford. Being a student I was not anxious to meet more professors than was strictly necessary. But out of politeness I said 'Yes, bring him along to my rooms tonight, we are having a meeting of the "Beef and Beer Club".' This was one of those serious undergraduates' debating societies that solved all the world's problems by smoking long pipes, drinking long beers and having long philosophic discussions.

Frank Buchman was brought to my rooms, a mysterious

stranger, his occupation unknown to us. Our curiosity was aroused. Frank was then a man of 42, of modest yet alert bearing, who seemed to take in everything around him and to feel perfectly at home. The rule of the club was that after the main papers had been read visitors were allowed to take part in the general discussion. We had been considering how to bring a change in the world, if possible by new political parties, scientific advance or international agreements. But as in Oxford we don't always stop talking when we have finished what we have to say, it was rather late before I had the chance to ask Frank Buchman for his comments. He said that he agreed with everything that had been said, in spite of the fact that violently contradictory opinions had been expressed. He added, 'Of course there has to be a change but that change might begin in people. For instance . . .' And he told us about two Cambridge undergraduates who had recently come to see him privately and had gone away deciding to be different. Naturally it was good news for us in Oxford to hear that Cambridge men were changing. Frank was too polite to tell us that we needed to change, but the people he told us about were so like ourselves, that he left us to draw our own conclusions. In my case these conclusions were highly uncomfortable and long overdue. I had been brought up in a strict Scottish home. That did not prevent me from committing sin, it only prevented me from enjoying it.

After Frank finished speaking, a silence fell. The atmosphere was changed. Up to then it had been comfortable, impersonal and academic. Now it was real, personal and slightly uncomfortable. Frank had not used any of the conventional religious phrases, but there was no doubt in the minds of anyone present what it was he was talking about. Religion was a subject that was barred from discussion in the club, except to sneer at it. A number of us were studying philosophy which has been described as a 'method of bewildering yourself systematically'. We had many theories, such as denying the existence of God and not believing that human nature could change. Jowett once defined tragedy as a beautiful hypothesis killed by a fact. Here was Frank Buchman presenting us with facts which killed most of our hypotheses stone-dead.

My room-mate was a Yorkshireman with red hair, who did not believe in God. I thought Sandy would not like what Dr. Buchman had said. But to my surprise Sandy suggested that we should invite Frank to breakfast next morning. I was a little nervous of inviting Frank to breakfast, because I thought he would try to change us, and it was too early in the morning. So we ordered a large breakfast to keep Frank busy eating, and give him as little chance as possible to ask any awkward questions. I need hardly say that this precaution proved totally unnecessary. We discussed the weather, cricket and all the conventional subjects of conversation, all the time knowing that the moment had to come when those subjects would be exhausted and anything might happen.

Frank told us about his recent travels in India and China and described how the headmistress of a school had asked him what he would do with a boy who had stolen money. Frank had said to the headmistress, 'When did you steal last?' The headmistress was honest and said 'I remember taking money from my father's desk when I was a girl.' Frank said, 'Will you tell that to your pupil?' The headmistress decided to do so. The result was change all around. While Frank was speaking I wondered why he should tell *us* that story. I knew a good many people to whom it would apply. When Frank finished speaking Sandy looked up and said, 'I have not always been honest about money.' This was a bit of a shock, as I come from Scotland, a country which feels very deeply about money. It did not surprise me that Sandy had been dishonest about money, but I was surprised that he admitted it to a man who was almost a total stranger. Then it was my turn to be honest, and I remembered some money I owed the college dance committee, having attended one of their dances without paying for the ticket. So I spent the rest of breakfast wondering whom I could borrow the money from, supposing I did decide to pay it back.

Inwardly I registered a vote of confidence in this man Frank Buchman. Little as I might agree with his theories, you could not help but feel his sincerity and power. Critical and snobbish as we were about people from other countries with other manners, even from other universities, yet Frank by his naturalness and simplicity immediately won his way without any attempt at 'making an impression'.

In the next few days it was extraordinary to find how many people were interested in that evening's discussion. People who were almost strangers to me, came up and asked about Frank Buchman, what he had said and how he looked, etc. And it was quite evident that a deep interest had been aroused. Among the most unlikely people to become interested in Frank was a young

man whom I once heard described as the most brilliant undergraduate in Oxford for ten years. He founded the Atheist Society
at Eton and continued it at Oxford. He used to hold public
meetings on Sunday afternoons at which leading Divines stated
the Christian case and were answered by our friend. On a show
of hands at the close of the debate our atheist friend usually won
by a comfortable majority. This presented a bit of a problem to
the Oxford authorities. When this young man heard that Frank
Buchman had arrived in Oxford and that Frank believed in the
Holy Spirit, our friend laughed and decided that he would argue
him out of such old-fashioned beliefs. So he invited Frank to his
room for coffee. That is where he made his first mistake. He found
that he could not get Frank to argue. For an hour he stated his
atheist beliefs, and the only response he could get was, 'Is that
so?' 'Do you really mean to say so?' 'Well, think of that.' Then
he asked Frank a surprising question. 'I wish you would tell me
just what you think of me.' Frank looked him in the eye and
said, 'You do not want me to be rude, do you?' The student
persisted in his demand, and Frank told him three things. He
said, 'First you are divided and at conflict in your mind.' Our
friend agreed. Then Frank said, 'You have an unhappy home.'
He agreed again. Then Frank told him that he needed help with
moral problems. He denied that, and said that he could control
himself. Frank did not argue. The clock struck midnight. Frank
said, 'I must go.' The student said, 'Do not go.' Frank said,
'I will stay on one condition, that you and I listen to God together.' Our atheist friend made a surprising reply. 'I could not
do that. I told you a lie a few minutes ago.' Frank said quite
cheerfully, 'I know you did.' Then the whole truth came out.
The interview ended on their knees.

The next day the young atheist did two things. He wrote
a letter of apology to his father, 'healing years of bitterness in
the home', and he scrapped an essay. He was considered one
of the most brilliant of the undergraduates, and had even been
offered a post to teach moral philosophy while still an undergraduate. In his thesis he outlined a new philosophy for post-
war England on the basis of atheistic humanism. His tutor,
who thought highly of his gifts, was very surprised when he
appeared in his study, put the uncompleted essay on the table
and said, 'We'll have to scrap all this.' His tutor said, 'Why?'
to which Dr. Buchman's convert replied, 'We are after the

highest truth we know, and the highest truth is that God has come into my life.'

Loudon Hamilton was offered a permanent appointment on the staff at Eton, a very tempting offer to a young man with practically no private means, for in those days with taxation at a moderate level, and the pound worth nearly three times what it is worth today, Eton offered, as it still does, not only a delightful life for those with a love of teaching, but also generous remuneration and financial security. Loudon Hamilton turned the offer down and has worked without salary ever since, worked with complete faith that 'Where God guides, He provides.'

The Oxford Group

MRAs are always careful to explain that the name 'Oxford Group' did not originate in the Group itself. When in 1928 seven men, six of them Oxonians, visited South Africa straight from Oxford the Press accordingly called them 'The Oxford Group'. 'The name,' we are assured, 'was soon riveted on them.' This is disingenuous. They were free either to accept this name or to reject it, as they had rejected 'Buchmanites'. If they had not liked the name they would not have adopted it.

The soundest defence is based on the admittedly close connection of the Oxford Group with Oxford University. The Oxford Group met every year at Oxford. The connection with Oxford was far closer than the connection of the Keswick Convention with Keswick. The overwhelming majority of the leaders of the movement were Oxonians, and the proportion of Oxonians in the Oxford Group was—in those early days—at least as high as the proportion of Oxonians in the Oxford Movement.

Sir Alan Herbert did all in his power to prevent the Board of Trade permitting this name to be used when the Movement was formally incorporated as an 'Association not for profit'. Sir Alan could count on the support of one sometime co-worker with the Oxford Group itself, Mr. H. Chalmers Bell, an advanced Anglo-Catholic. In his little book *Catholics and the Group Movement*, Mr. Bell wrote:

The *fons et origo* of the Group was Keswick: an earlier scene of
its activity than Oxford was Cambridge. Its present headquarters
are in London. It is to be feared that the adoption of this acci-
dentally conferred title is an instance of the sacrifice of truth
to a sense of its value as publicity. It would pass if we were not
so particular about 'absolute honesty'; but in face of the Group
teaching the title should be quietly dropped.

Dr. Hensley Henson, Bishop of Durham, quoted this in a
letter to *The Times* (8th June 1939), and in the same issue
Lord Hugh Cecil, an Oxford graduate and at one time Burgess
for the University in the House of Commons, defended the
use of the name 'Oxford Group'. Lord Hugh asked:

> Are Mr. Herbert's feelings outraged when his bootmaker speaks
> of 'Oxford shoes'? Or are mine (as Provost) offended when a
> hosier talks of 'Eton collars'? Or does it distress any member of
> the Royal Family when he hears of 'Windsor soap'?

To which somebody should, but nobody did reply that in the
cases cited there was no possible room for misunderstanding.
Nobody, for instance, has ever suspected the Royal Family of
engaging in the manufacture of soap. But on the Continent at
least, the Oxford Group is often confused with Newman's
Oxford Movement, and even in England the name suggests
as close a connection of the Oxford Group with the University
as existed in the case of the Oxford Movement.

The Times Literary Supplement (16th March 1933) expressed
what most Oxford men, including the present writer, felt:

> There is no valid reason for including 'Oxford' in its title; and
> the reasons against it are particularly strong at a time when the
> centenary of the real Oxford Movement is about to be observed,
> for it would be difficult to find Christian methods and ideals
> more widely divergent than those of Dr. Buchman's disciples and
> those of the Tractarians.

It was indeed rash to invite a comparison, if only by implication, with the Oxford Movement, because the contrast, if
judged only by aesthetic criteria, was shattering. Inevitably
one compared the noblest cadences of Newman's prose with
the manifestos of the Group, and, unfairly perhaps, Newman's

hymn, *Lead, kindly light,* with a rhyme which Mrs. Sheed heard more than once during a house party at Oxford.

> It's not an institution
> It's not a point of view,
> It starts a revolution
> By starting one in you.

The name 'Oxford Group', which was at first an asset, became a liability when the movement began to recruit its disciples in every continent and in every class. For a world-wide movement it was clearly a handicap to be identified, if only by name, with a particular class and a particular university in a particular country. The name 'Oxford Group' is now retained solely for legal purposes in England and the movement is now known as 'Moral Re-Armament'.

A House Party at Interlaken

It was on 29th May 1938 that Dr. Buchman launched the Oxford Group's campaign for Moral Re-Armament at a meeting in the East Ham Town Hall. In July of the same year my wife and I, at the invitation of old ski-ing friends, Mr. and Mrs. E. T. C. Milligan, attended a 'House Party' at Interlaken.

The Czech crisis was acute. War seemed all but inevitable, if not in that same summer at least before long. England was not as yet awakened to the danger that threatened her. Even after Hitler had annexed Prague the Socialists and Liberals voted against conscription. I knew that England's immediate need, if we were to survive, was material re-armament, and though of course there was no need to choose between moral and material re-armament, there was something disconcertingly remote and unrealistic about the atmosphere of the Interlaken 'House Party'. What was the use, I felt, of a Sudeten German talking about the urgent need to 'change' both the Germans and the Czechs, if war were to be avoided? Was there, I asked, the remotest possibility of 'changing' Hitler? And, if not, what was the duty of Christians in a world in which, as we were soon to discover, Hitler and Stalin were at that very moment planning to 'share' Poland?

Little that was said, either on the platform or elsewhere,

appealed to me. I remember in particular one remark made by a lady who was well-born and wealthy, a remark which only by an excess of charity could be described as tasteless. A rotten egg is not tasteless.

On the other hand I was impressed not only by the shattering sincerity of our friends the Milligans, but also by the enigma of M.R.A., its appeal to many whose aesthetic consciences, I felt, must have been acutely disturbed. I remember a graduate from my old college, Balliol, Bernard Hallward, who had won a D.S.O. and whose career had been distinguished. 'You can,' he said, 'riddle all this and Dr. Buchman's manifestos with criticism, as I did when I first came into contact with it, and yet such criticisms only scratch the surface. You've got to explain the strength of the attraction which can overcome those prejudices which keep you, and which nearly kept me, out of the Oxford Group.'

And I was conscious as he spoke of an unsolved enigma. The idiom of M.R.A. might be dissuasive, but even so I could not help uneasily suspecting that this movement had been called into being to serve a divine purpose.

Two years later, just after Dunkirk, I met a Cork priest who summed up his own bewildered reaction to events in a sentence which I have never forgotten. 'Sure it *does* seem that God is using the British for His purpose, and it is not for us to question His taste in instruments.' I felt much the same about the Oxford Group.

I described the Interlaken 'House Party' in a book which was written five years later, *The Good Gorilla*. My prejudices against M.R.A. had been strengthened by the War during which I crossed the Atlantic six times. In November 1940 I went to the U.S.A. to lecture on the Battle of Britain and crossed America from coast to coast four times before returning to England.

I now know that British members of the Oxford Group in America were rendering a service to their country, and that almost all the British MRAs of military age were in the Services. At the time I only knew that the British Group in America were of military age and that Dr. Buchman, who had been glad enough for his work to be identified with Oxford in times of peace, carefully avoided any overt encouragement to those Americans who were campaigning for intervention to save the country which had provided Dr. Buchman with most of his lieutenants and with a name for his movement. I am explaining not defending my prejudices, prejudices which were derived from a misconception of M.R.A., for it is not the function of M.R.A. to sponsor or endorse any particular nationality or political policy, but rather to persuade men to seek God's guidance.

I hope that I have not been wholly unsuccessful in putting into practice the principles of honest controversy as defined on page 16 of this book, but my chapter on the Interlaken 'House Party' was certainly a sorry lapse from those standards. I should have written to the headquarters of M.R.A. in London to discover their defence against the charges which were being broadcast at the time, as for instance that Dr. Buchman had exclaimed, 'Thank God for Adolf Hitler', or that Bunny Austin and young MRAs were dodging military service by staying on in America. I must defer for the moment the answers to these accusations and merely express my regret that I did not elicit those answers before writing my chapter.

Though the chapter in which I described the 'House Party' was hostile and unjust, there is evidence in the book of my ambivalent attitude to M.R.A. Chapter IX, for instance, was clearly intended to modify the views expressed in Chapter II. The Communists were delighted by Chapter II and for some years it was their practice to circulate long extracts from this chapter to the Catholic clergy in any town (as for instance in India) which an M.R.A. mission was about to visit. These extracts, I am told, 'did immense harm'.

My friends the Milligans had every right to be incensed by the use which I made of my experiences at the 'House Party', to which they had introduced me, but they bore no malice. On the contrary, Milligan startled me by refusing to send in a bill for a minor operation. Thanks to his surgical skill there has been no recurrence of my 'first fine careless rupture'.

The immediate effect of his magnanimity was to reinforce an uneasy feeling that I had done less than justice to M.R.A., and I was therefore predisposed to accept an invitation to spend a week-end at Caux. That was in 1953. I was met at the station by Mr. Robert Readhead, a skier and the father of a ski-ing friend Colonel Robert Readhead. That week-end was the first of many, many visits during the last four years.

It is perhaps hardly necessary to explain that Caux is reached by a cog railway from Montreux on Lake Geneva. It was once a fashionable spring and autumn centre, but even before the Second World War the Palace Hotel was losing money. All the hotels in Caux are now owned by M.R.A., and the former Palace Hotel is known as Mountain House.

IV

THE DAY'S ROUND AT CAUX

THE MRAs are early risers. Many of them set their alarm clocks for 5 a.m., few for later than 6 a.m., in order to devote at least an hour to their 'Quiet Time'.

Quiet Time and Guidance

The essence of M.R.A. is summed up in a passage often quoted in their pamphlets:

> The world does not change because you do not change. But the world can change if you change. How can you change? By listening to God, for God is always speaking. Just as the sun is always shining. In the morning before the distractions and problems of the day you can listen to God. How can you listen? Here is the answer. You write it down. Write it down so that you can listen better and you can remember His words.

Am I quoting Dr. Buchman? I am not. These words were written by a Catholic priest, Father Gratry, a French Oratorian, in his book, *Les Sources*. He died about a hundred years ago, by an odd coincidence at Glion within sight of Caux, the Swiss headquarters of M.R.A.

Once when I made a very early call on an MRA, before catching the first train down to Montreux, I found him sitting up in bed with a notebook in his hands. An MRA would be as lost without his notebook as a priest without his Breviary. Into this notebook go the thoughts that have come to him during his 'Quiet Time'. They are written down, because 'the strongest memory is weaker than the palest ink'. MRAs always withdraw for a 'Quiet Time' before any important decision is taken.

There is often a class for Bible students at about 6.30 a.m., and there is always a meeting about 7.30 a.m., the object of which is primarily to plan the day's programme, and to invite suggestions for speakers at the two Assemblies (morning and afternoon). An important guest (unchanged) is arriving. What line should the Assembly take to change him? If the guest were an English Member of Parliament, Mr. John McGovern, M.P., might be asked to open the Assembly. Then there are the routine chores. A dozen men are needed to help unload some new equipment for the cinema. 'Any volunteers?' says the leader of the meeting. Forty hands shoot up and twelve are chosen by the leader of the meeting.

This first meeting, which every MRA attends who is not otherwise occupied in some work for the common good, for instance preparing breakfast, is followed by a smaller meeting of those whose special task it is to plan in some detail the topics to be discussed at the Assemblies, and to select the platform speakers.

Sharing

At breakfast you will often see a group of MRAs with their little notebooks open. They are 'Sharing' and checking their 'Guidance', the 'Guidance' received during the 'Quiet Time' must be checked.

Firstly, with reference to the four absolute standards:

> Absolute Honesty
> Absolute Purity
> Absolute Unselfishness
> Absolute Love.

Secondly, with reference to the religious teachings of their respective faiths.

Thirdly, by sharing their 'Guidance' received in 'Quiet Time' with friends.

Often the group that meet to 'share' their 'Guidance' consists of an informal team. There are advantages in the same team meeting day by day as they gradually develop an expert knowledge of the particular problems of the particular group.

A Belgian Dominican who joined one of these teams for a week told me that he had been greatly impressed by the similarity of their approach to the spiritual advice so often given in Catholic retreats. 'There was an honesty and a humility

about their self-criticisms, and a lack of vanity in the way
they accepted criticisms from other members of the team
which was truly edifying.'

And apart from the regular teams which meet to discuss
their spiritual problems, there are teams for every activity connected with Caux. If you wander through Mountain House
during the day you will often find little groups of silent MRAs
with their notebooks handy to record 'Guidance'. They may
be planning a menu for dinner, or the best approach to some
visitor whom they are trying to 'change'.[1]

Assemblies

There are normally two Assemblies every day, the first at
11 a.m. and the second at 5 p.m. As the big hall begins to
fill up a pianist plays gay music. The speakers are on the platform. If, to take one example, the theme to be discussed is
Africa, a characteristic selection of speakers would be a Nigerian
Member of Parliament, an African from Kenya, a South
African of Dutch and a South African of British descent, and
behind the speakers the massed choir.

The Mackinac singers (so-called because M.R.A. assemblies are held every year on Mackinac Island in Lake Michi-
gan) are very effective. Immense trouble is taken in the
selection and still more in the training of the choir. Even
Mr. Geoffrey Williamson, a hostile witness, can write of them
in his book, *Inside Buchmanism*:

> Most people appreciate fine singing, and the Mackinac Singers
> give of their best. Though they have performed a thousand times,
> their zeal is in no way diminished. Their diction is faultless and
> every song is 'put over' with a gusto which seems spontaneous.
> Their vitality seems unflagging.

Special songs of welcome have been written for different
professions and nations. A Welsh miner's speech from the platform might be introduced by the Rhondda song, an M.P. by

[1] I shall dispense in future with inverted commas when I use MRA terms,
'share', 'guidance'. 'quiet time' and 'change', for the inverted commas have an
irritant effect on MRA readers, perhaps because too often offensive or at least
sceptical innuendos are intended by such use.

the Westminster song. National delegations are always welcomed in their own national anthem.

M.R.A. is often criticised for the careful planning of these effects. I wonder why? The great religions have all reinforced their appeal to heart and mind by the appeal to the emotions through music and art.

The usual plan is to translate English speeches into German or French or vice versa, but every member of the audience is provided with earphones which connect by short wave radio with translators in an alcove above the Hall. The languages into which the speeches will be translated are announced on a notice board. The ordinary European languages present no difficulty, and where necessary speeches can be translated into Japanese, Arabic or Turkish.

The Plays

After dinner the big theatre is normally full to overflowing. It is here that plays are performed and M.R.A. films shown. The same system of earphones is used for the plays as for the Assemblies.

Such then is the Day's Round. A dull but necessary chapter, for no intelligent discussion of Caux is possible until the basic routine is grasped.

There are two more questions which every visitor to Caux asks. How is M.R.A. run, and where does the money come from? I shall do my best to answer these questions in my next chapter.

V

ORGANISATION AND FINANCE

Organism

MRAs always insist that M.R.A. is not an organisation but an organism. An organism, however, which owns property must appoint some central body legally competent to administer funds and to receive bequests. It was therefore decided that the most suitable means for the Oxford Group to become a legal entity would be by way of incorporation as an 'Association not for profit', in accordance with the Companies Act (1929).

The need for incorporation was emphasised in 1938-39 by a case in the High Court (Thackrah v. Wilson) where a bequest left to the Oxford Group was held to be invalid on the ground that it was not a legally identifiable body, though the work was known throughout the world by that name. In 1939 the Oxford Group was incorporated, and officially recognised as a charity in March 1951.

The incorporated Oxford Group has a Council of Management of seventeen members, who are responsible not only for administration, which the Group has always kept to the essential minimum, but also for the direction and policy of every aspect of the work of the Group. In exercising this responsibility, the Council draws on the wide experience of the full-time workers, and most of the Council are themselves full-time workers of long standing with experience of the Group's work in every part of the world.

The property of M.R.A. in other countries is similarly administered. These Councils of Management in England and in other countries are not elected, for M.R.A. has no life members and no subscription. New members are co-opted when necessary to fill vacancies.

Of organisation, in the sense of direction from above, there is very little at Caux or in any other M.R.A. centre, and indeed it is difficult for the casual visitor to realise, and at first almost impossible for him to believe, how completely the MRAs rely on guidance. No directives, for instance, are ever issued to teams in distant parts.

I am often asked what will happen when Dr. Buchman dies. 'Who will be his successor?' There will be no official successor. Even today Dr. Buchman's position is unofficial, a primacy of honour rather than of constitutional status. I remember, during a prolonged absence of Dr. Buchman from Caux, asking Lionel Jardine whether there had been any formal appointment of a deputy to take the chair at the important planning meetings. 'There has been no such appointment. Paul Campbell led the meeting this morning, and if in my guidance I had been convinced that I was the proper person to take the chair, and said so to Campbell, he would have agreed.'

Finance

There is no mystery about the finances of M.R.A. In a letter to *The Times* on 13th October 1953, Sir Lynden Macassey stated in reply to a critic who had talked about the 'secret finances' of the Group:

> M.R.A. in the United Kingdom is incorporated as the Oxford Group. Its audited accounts are lodged annually with the Board of Trade. They show for the year ended 31st March 1953, £80,796 as the income of the United Kingdom association, which includes sales of literature £24,725 and gifts £54,535. Of the gifts, forty-three per cent were under £10, forty-eight per cent between £10 and £99, and nine per cent were £100 or more. Gifts from industrial firms were less than three per cent of the total income. The accounts of M.R.A. as incorporated in other countries follow the same pattern.

The Oxford Group's accounts are audited annually by Messrs. Price, Waterhouse and Company, Chartered Accountants, of 3 Frederick Place, Old Jewry, London, E.C.2.

The finances of M.R.A. are not, as the critic in *The Times* suggested, 'secret'. They are public—and mysterious. Mysterious, that is, to those who are not prepared to accept the principle on which MRAs act with shattering conviction, that 'Where God guides He provides'. An MRA with no private means and no salary marries a penniless girl and somehow or other they never want for the necessities of life, food, clothing and shelter. Dr. Buchman is guided to send 135 MRAs round the world, and charters planes long before there is any concrete evidence that the money for so fantastically expensive a project will be forthcoming. And in due course the 'guided' are also provided for. The bill for the planes on the 1955 world mission was $124,930, that is over £40,000.

M.R.A. has some regular sources of income. Nearly two million copies of Peter Howard's books have been sold, the royalties on which have accrued to M.R.A., but most of the money is the fruit of sacrificial giving.

On one occasion when I stopped at the M.R.A. centre in Bonn I asked if I could see their monthly accounts. My host, David Lancashire, went into another room and returned with the accounts. The subscribers were almost all little people who gave little sums but often regular sums of money. A domestic servant gave three marks (about five shillings) a month, and so on.

Here are some typical extracts from their books in their London Headquarters.

M.P.	£2
East London Mayor	£10
Accountant	£50
Officer	£194 15s. 10d.
Typist	10s.
Clergyman	£1
Welsh playwright	£50
Bus driver	15s.
Doctor	£100
Miners' leader	£1
L.C.C. employee	£1
Children's nurse	£10
Exporting firm	£500
Railway executive	£5
Masseuse	£7
55 workers	£37 2s. 6d.
Captain, R.N.	£25

Privy Councillor . . .	£2
Engineering Company . .	£1000
Head, Oxford College . .	£10
Kenya farmer	£250
Headmaster	£49
Textile employee . . .	£25

An analysis of the regular givers (those giving under covenant) in Britain showed that 12 per cent of the covenants were given by teachers; 23 per cent by doctors and other professional men and women; 6 per cent by members or retired members of the forces; 27 per cent by businessmen ranging from directors of large firms to shopkeepers; 13 per cent by housewives.

In Switzerland in the last financial year 20 per cent of the gifts were of 20 francs or under; 40 per cent between 20 and 100 francs, and 40 per cent upwards of 100 francs.

'The Economics of Christ'

The full-time workers receive no salary and depend entirely on 'the economics of Christ'. They are fond of quoting our Lord's instructions to the Twelve when He sent them forth on their first missionary journey:

> Provide neither gold, nor silver, nor brass in your purses, nor scrip for your journey, neither two coats, neither shoes, nor yet staves, for the labourer is worthy of his hire.

In the authoritative book *The Oxford Group and its Work of Moral Re-Armament* to which Sir Lynden Macassey, K.B.E., Q.C., LL.D., contributes a foreword, the guiding principles of the Oxford Group are thus set forth: 'Suppose everybody cared enough, everybody shared enough, wouldn't everybody have enough? There is enough in the world for everyone's need but not enough for everyone's greed.'

This principle, enunciated by Dr. Buchman from the outset of his work, is and always has been the economic creed of the Oxford Group. It is, in fact, the modern version of early apostolic practice described by St. Luke: 'None of them that believed said that any of the things that he possessed was his own.'

From its first beginnings the Group has advanced through the sacrificial giving of those who believe in its mission. People have given of their wages, their capital, their houses, their jewellery, their savings to the furtherance of the work.

During the months that I spent at Caux I seldom lunched or dined twice with the same group. My friend Garth Lean knew that I was writing a book and was anxious to meet full-time workers. Newman distinguishes between the nominal assent that we give to beliefs which we are not prepared to reject but in which we acquiesce without enthusiasm, and the real assent when we are completely convinced. At first my assent to the claim that M.R.A. is financed by faith was nominal rather than real, but it was impossible to resist the cumulative effect of life stories, the details of which varied but the underlying pattern of which was the same.

There was, for instance, the case of Mary Gaddie who became a full-time worker in 1932. Her first assignment was Gateshead-on-Tyne, where she arrived with £5 in her pocket and left three months later with £5. A friend provided a bed and three meals a day. She needed a new dress. Somebody gave her material and then a day or two later a dressmaking friend, whom she had not seen for some time, turned up and offered to make her a dress. Meanwhile she had to provide not only for herself but for a sick mother who needed a nurse in the house when, as happened from time to time, Mary Gaddie was on an assignment. Somehow or other the necessary money always turned up, like intermittent manna from heaven.

Her initial capital of £5 having been increased in the course of twenty years to £8, she felt that she could give £5 to help finance a team in India. Next day somebody sent her a cheque for £3 which she gave to an MRA going to Australia. Then she herself was invited to go to Denmark. She needed a new dress and money for a ticket, both of which were forthcoming, just in time. M.R.A., by the way, very rarely provides fares[1] when an MRA is assigned to some distant station. If God has guided then God will provide for them. And the fantastic fact is that He does.

[1] It is only exceptionally that a plane is chartered.

Take the case of a Danish girl, Inge Johansen. She came from a poor home and joined the Communist party, and both she and her brother were active in the Resistance Movement. Then she met M.R.A. and became a full-time worker. 'I was so poor,' she said, 'that I had to sell my books to attend an M.R.A. Assembly. Then my mother fell ill. I was in Italy at the time and I wondered whether I ought not to take a job in Denmark and help support my mother, but my guidance was to continue my work with the team in Italy. I talked the matter over with the team and this thought came to me in guidance, "You trust God to provide for you and for the world work of M.R.A. Can't you have faith that God will look after your mother through you?" On that very day, as the postmark proved, a friend of mine in M.R.A. wrote to offer me her monthly income of 100 Swiss francs. "I don't know," she wrote, "what the money is for, but my guidance is to send it to you." '

God may provide, but He does not provide more than is strictly necessary. An example from my own experience is worth quoting. I fell ill while I was at Caux with a parathoid gland infection, and was looked after by a Dutch doctor who had abandoned a promising career to devote his life to M.R.A. Dr. Harro Begemann made a deep impression on me. He was the embodiment of *Sancta simplicitas*. Simplicity and goodness. It would have been wholly contrary to the traditions of M.R.A. to send me in a bill, and when I handed the doctor a cheque made out to him, he said, 'Thank you so much. We badly need some more equipment.'

'Perhaps,' I replied, 'but this cheque is for you. "People," as you are fond of saying here, "are more important than things." It's you and the nurses that I'm grateful to, not "things", thermometers, injection syringes, etc.'

He looked immensely relieved. 'My boots,' he said, 'are wearing out, and I was praying that somebody would be guided to give me enough money to buy a new pair.' And yet in spite of his obvious need for new boots he would have spent the cheque on medical equipment unless I had insisted that it was intended for the *personal* needs of himself and the nurses.

It is not only the individuals who live by faith, but M.R.A. as a whole. No summer passes without a crisis of unpaid bills. and when the crisis becomes acute, Dr. Buchman summons his lieutenants to a special session of prayer. Dr. Buchman never budgets before planning a missionary journey to distant lands. He decides on an itinerary which comes to him in guidance, informs the towns he proposes to visit, say Colombo, Madras, Karachi, etc., that he will be there on such and such a date. And he then waits patiently for Providence to finance a charter plane and hospitality en route.

What would happen, I often ask myself, if a 'Task Force', to use their terminology, found itself in Africa or India without resources and no means of getting home? I put this question to Loudon Hamilton. 'It's always happening,' he said cheerfully. 'In Nigeria, for instance, last year we had run out of money and there were still the air passages to buy to the next place. The only thing to do was to get down on our benders and pray hard.' So they got down on their benders and the money essential for their needs turned up, as apparently it always does. Only just enough money, and only just in time.

In one case a registered letter may reach a team from an MRA who has been left a legacy which he places at their disposal, or another MRA may have gone to live at M.R.A. headquarters in London and sold his house in order to help the team in Africa, or an officer decides to give his war gratuity.

So far, at least, the necessary manna has always been forthcoming, and a fiasco has always been avoided. But suppose the supply of providential manna ran short . . . supposing the Consuls had to finance the return passages of stranded and destitute apostles of M.R.A. . . . . It is easy to imagine the contemptuous comments by enemies of M.R.A., and the kind of article which might be written on the theme 'Where God guides, the taxpayer provides'. Every time Dr. Buchman launches a team on some distant land he is risking a humiliating fiasco. I do not know which I admire most, his imperturbable faith or his iron nerve.

M.R.A. is kept going by sacrificial giving on a scale for which I know there are precedents, but which is sufficiently unusual to startle those who have taken the trouble to look into M.R.A. finances. The longer I stayed at Caux the greater my admiration for this scale of sacrificial giving. Many MRAs give a tenth or more of their income to help the full-time workers. A retired Civil Servant admitted to me that he had just given M.R.A. £1,000. His children, it seemed, raised no objection, but if I were a young man I would do all in my power to keep my parents from Caux, for avarice, though an objectionable quality in oneself, is the most desirable quality in one's immediate and more distant ancestors.

I was at Caux on 7th August 1955, when funds were collected to send the all-African cast of the play *Freedom* to various capitals in Europe. On this particular Sunday morning Caux had unpaid bills in the neighbourhood of 150,000 francs (over £12,000). Dr. Buchman, none the less, announced that the cast would leave for London. 5,830 Swiss francs were collected at that particular Assembly, 62,470 Swiss francs were promised, and the jewellery handed up to the platform was valued at 20,000 Swiss francs. Thus more than the equivalent of £7,000 was collected or promised from one Assembly.

A constant stream of donors came to the platform. A Cairo University student, Abdulla el Maamoon Abu Shusha, said, 'I have nothing but only what I have here. I have only got a watch which was my father's. I lost him a couple of months ago.' As he took the watch off his wrist he concluded by saying, 'Here I give you a part of my heart and a part of my memories.'

A young Australian architect, Ronald Pratt, said, 'I went to the Gold Coast to make money there and take money away. I give this now to put *Freedom* on the road.'

An English lady, Mrs. Irene Smith, the widow of a Manchester surgeon, whose father had made a fortune from shares in the mines and industries of the world, said, 'I will sell jewels made from Africa's gold and precious stones. My heart goes with the Africans as they find their true destiny in remaking the world.' Furthermore, she announced that she would give an annuity of £2,000.

'Africa is giving Britain another chance to change,' said an English school teacher, Miss Dorothy Rant, who was giving the proceeds from the sale of her house to help present *Freedom*. 'I wanted to keep this money for my old age, but now I realise that money is no security. True security lies in a hate-free and greed-free world.'

One of the delegation selected to represent Alexandria University at the World Assembly gave his watch. 'This watch was given me as a reward by my professor in the university.' The leader, Dr. Riad Halwagy, spoke on behalf of the delegation and declared that they intended on their return journey to Egypt to forgo lunch and dinner to contribute to the launching of *Freedom*.

From Lapland a high school headmaster and his wife, Mr. and Mrs. Wallmark, gave 500 kroner and a diamond ring. He said, 'A man who is prepared to give his heart and all he has is part of the cure for the world.'

'As a symbol of my apologies for the way my country has lived and as a symbol of the new alliance between our continents, I give this family ring,' said the French editor, Philip Schweisguth.

A ring worth a million French francs was given by a Brazilian baroness, Baroness de Flaghac. A Dutch business man with a family of six gave ten thousand guilders. A pearl necklace, treasured because of its family associations, was unclasped by a young Canadian girl, Miss Margaret Fleming, and handed to the chairman of the meeting.

I remember a luncheon party at which I was asked for my views about Caux, and I replied that what impressed me most was the calm way in which Dr. Buchman assumed that the money he needed would somehow turn up. Somebody present said, 'Don't you believe it. Buchman's got some hidden resources somewhere.' But a well-known Catholic priest dissented, 'I'm not particularly surprised by what you tell me. There are many precedents for Religious Communities who adopted the same method of financing by faith.' And not only religious communities.

'Where God guides, He provides' was the guiding principle in the life of George Müller, who died in 1898, and whose story is told in *The Life of Trust: being a Narrative of the Lord's Dealings with George Müller*, a book from which there are long quotations in William James's *The Varieties of Religious Experience*.

Müller, in the course of his life, distributed two million copies of the scriptures, equipped several hundred missionaries, built five large orphanages in America in which he educated 121,000 orphans. He received and administered a million and a half pounds sterling, and left at the age of eighty-six an estate worth £160. Müller never ran up bills and never bought supplies for which he could not pay on the spot. God provided, but only just what was needed and only just in time.

> Greater and more manifest nearness of the Lord's presence I have never had than when after breakfast there were no means for dinner for more than a hundred persons; or when after dinner there were no means for the tea, and yet the Lord provided the tea; and all this without one single human having been informed of our need.

Müller always refused to borrow money for any of his enterprises:

> How does it work when we thus anticipate God by going our own way? We certainly weaken faith instead of increasing it; and each time we work thus a deliverance of our own we find it more and more difficult to trust in God, till at last we give way entirely to our own fallen reason and unbelief prevails.

When supplies came in slowly Müller always felt that this was a trial of his faith. When his faith and patience had been sufficiently tried God would send more:

> And this has been proved, for to-day was given me the sum of £2,050 of which £2,000 are for the building fund and £50 for present necessities. It is impossible to describe my joy in God when I received this donation. I was neither excited nor surprised; for I *look out* for answers to my prayers.

I have cited Müller's experience to emphasise an important point. Nobody in M.R.A. has ever suggested that they are the first, or among the first, to practise 'the economics of Christ', nor for that matter the first to inspire heroic self-sacrifice. All that they do claim is that the M.R.A. way of life is a striking vindication of an ancient truth, the fact that 'Where God

D

guides, He provides', a principle which has often been tested and which, so they insist, has never failed.

A question often asked by critics of M.R.A. is whether the best use is made of the sums thus raised. 'Why should not teams travel by cargo boats?' is a characteristic and not unreasonable comment. Nearly two hundred MRAs travelled round the world in 1955, visiting among other places, Formosa, Japan, Burma, Siam, India, Kenya, Egypt and Turkey. Howard's play *The Vanishing Island* was given in all these countries. Clearly the most efficient way in which to transport the actors and other members of what M.R.A. described as 'The World Mission' was to charter planes, and this was done. In a later chapter I give my reasons for supposing that the headquarters in London and at Caux are run without waste and indeed with the greatest attention to economy.

VI

CONTRASTS

THE chairman called on a young man in the twenties to address the Assembly. 'I came here a week ago,' he began, 'because a friend of mine invited me, and I was inquisitive about M.R.A. and delighted to visit Switzerland. I considered myself to be a pretty fair to average Christian. I said my prayers and went to church now and then, but Caux has taught me that I have been so far completely ineffective. From now on I'm going to live by the four absolute standards . . .'

The effect produced on me was much as if a young man had announced that henceforth he had decided to go in for heroic virtue. 'Why don't you encourage people,' I asked, 'to talk about *aiming* at Absolute Love, etc., instead of announcing that they're going to live by those standards?'

'Because,' said Howard, 'if I may say to myself I'm going to *aim* at a standard I have reconciled myself in advance to failing, whereas if I assure myself that I'm going to live absolute standards, then I am humiliated by my failure and that incites me to do better.'

I saw his point. A Catholic who confesses some besetting sin may have little doubt but that he will fall again, but none the less he leaves the confessional with a 'firm purpose of amendment' the effect of which should at least increase the intervals between sinning.

'Nobody,' Peter Howard continued, 'who shares his thoughts with others in M.R.A. could possibly entertain for a moment the idea that he had achieved perfection. We don't spare ourselves or our friends when we share our guidance.' It is the candid criticism which is part of the routine of sharing which insures M.R.A. against the recurrent danger of perfectionism, a recurring symptom in the history of Enthusiasm.

By perfectionism I do not mean aiming at perfection, which is a duty binding on all Christians, 'Be ye therefore perfect, even as your Father which is in heaven is perfect.' (St. Matt. 5:48.) Perfectionism is the technical name given to the illusion that perfection has actually been attained. Thus Henry Nicholas, the Dutch founder of the Familists, said that 'God raised him up, anointed him with his Godly being and goaded him with himself.' Vitell, his English disciple, was credited with the assertion that the godly do not sin, and ought not to use a prayer in which they describe themselves as miserable sinners. Wesley never used the phrase 'sinless perfection', which was invented by Whitefield, but as Monsignor Knox rightly says, 'the language of Wesley's own followers was certainly arresting enough'. As for instance, 'I never find any cloud between God and me; I walk in the light continually', or Dorothy King who 'felt an entire change, while these words were spoken to her heart. "Thou art all fair, my love; there is no spot in thee".'

Though an occasional convert to M.R.A. may use language which seems tainted by perfectionism, the movement itself is wholly free from this error.

Absolute Love

God alone is absolute and though admittedly a standard must be absolute and unchanging to be of any value, even the greatest of saints can only approach the divine absolute. We can, however, begin to understand something of the implications of 'Absolute Love' by reading the lives of the saints.

There is a great devotion to St. Francis of Assisi at Caux, and I am sure that every MRA would recognise in Father Jean-Marie Vianney, the Curé d'Ars, an example almost as inspiring as that of St. Francis. Father Vianney was the dunce of the Seminary and was admitted to ordination only because there was such a shortage of vocations. He was given the poorest and wildest parish in the diocese, the remote parish of Ars, a village of two hundred souls.

His first act on taking possession of his parish, in 1818, was to—

take the furniture out of the rectory, give back tables and arm-
chairs to the gentry who had loaned them, distribute the rest to
the poor of the village, and retire for the night to the attic where
he lay down on the bare boards with a bundle of wood for his
pillow . . . Gradually he contrived almost to forgo sleep and
food. He neglected himself in illness and got rid of a severe
toothache by having the tooth taken out by the blacksmith with
a pair of pincers. He never spent a penny on himself; his clothes
and his food came from charity, and he distributed to the poor
even the money that had been given him to pay his doctor's
fees—he told the physician not to call as he could not pay for
the visit. Not only did he refuse riches, he refused honours as
well. There are abundant instances of this.[1]

A complete detachment from what Burke calls 'the solemn
plausibilities of this world' is a note of sanctity. I attended
a birthday party of Dr. Buchman's in London where the
various decorations which Eastern Governments had recently
bestowed on him were laid out on a table. I am sure that Dr.
Buchman values these decorations less as a tribute to himself
than as a tribute to the movement, but even so I could not
help recalling the Curé d'Ars giving away the Legion of
Honour to his curate, 'because it will give him greater pleasure
than it will me', as if it were an ordinary present which could
be given away to someone else. When he was made a canon,
the canon's mozetta had to be put on him by force. In the
evening he sold it for fifty francs, the price of the cloth, in
order to enable him to help a poor man.

It is the Curé d'Ars that I recall whenever I hear from
M.R.A. platforms confident references to the Four Absolutes,
and perhaps like so many Catholic critics of M.R.A. I find it
pleasanter to compare my friends in M.R.A. to the Curé
d'Ars than to compare myself to those who have sacrificed
career and salary to join that unselfish company, the full-time
workers at Caux.

' "Sorry" is a magic little word'
Contrast is the keynote to Caux in general, and to the

[1] *Miracles*, pp. 20-3, in the English translation of Jean Helle's book, published
by Burns and Oates.

Assemblies in particular. I have heard speeches from that platform which were deeply moving, and I have also sat through puerilities such as those recorded by Mr. Williamson in his book, *Inside Buchmanism*:

> More testimony followed from a group of sisters, who prompted their recollections by consulting little black note-books. One by one, with the utmost gravity, they 'confessed' to petty jealousies of each other's looks. 'I used to be very jealous of my sisters because I thought people took more notice of them than me' is a fair sample of the kind of thing to which that vast international gathering was obliged to listen that morning. I thought it an affront to busy statesmen and other distinguished guests, a waste of their valuable time and an imposition on their tolerance.

MRAs have brought about many a reconciliation by insisting that there is nothing so disarming as a candid apology, and that the way to heal a quarrel is not to try to awaken in the other man a conviction of sin, but to begin by admitting one's own errors. ' "Sorry" is a magic little word.' All that is very true, and there are occasions when one should give publicity to an apology. I am, for instance, glad to place on record in this book my regret, which I also conveyed privately to Dr. Buchman, for having given currency, in my first account of the Groups, to a libel which I now know to be without foundation, the charge that Dr. Buchman described Himmler as 'a great lad'. I was present at Caux when a public apology was so obviously spontaneous and so shatteringly sincere that everybody was deeply moved, as for instance when a German apologised for all the misery that the Nazis had inflicted on the occupied countries. Some of these apologies were, however, faintly funny. I remember a charming Vaudois girl apologising to the Bernese because, as a Vaudois, she had always considered herself culturally the superior of the Bernese. I did not myself feel that this particular apology would improve Vaudois-Bernese relations.[1]

[1] A friend of mine who has read the typescript of this book adds a pencilled footnote at this point: 'Is there not a sharp distinction between admitting a personal sin and publicly apologising, without their authority, for a group to which the apologiser may happen to belong? This 'group apology' is one of the things I find most distasteful about M.R.A.'

The public apology on Caux platforms has now become such a routine, so much an integral part of the M.R.A. tradition that it has ceased to be effective, except in very rare cases. It has acquired a quasi-liturgical status, but only *quasi*. Nobody resents stereotyped phrases which have been incorporated in a fixed liturgy. When the priest at Mass begins the *Confiteor*, the server does not murmur crossly, 'The same old stuff again. Bet he doesn't really mean it.' But something like that was my reaction more than once to what sounded like the kind of routine apology which the liturgy of M.R.A. required.

I soon wearied of hearing Englishmen apologising to Asiatics and Africans for British Imperialism, and I sympathised with a former Governor of the Sudan who exclaimed to me, 'The young fool who talked about the blood bath in Ashanti, for which he blamed us, might remember that before the Englishmen came to Ashanti blood baths and human sacrifices were routine.'

I look forward to seeing some Red Indians at Caux, if only for the pleasure of hearing Dr. Buchman apologise for the British Imperialism which expelled the Red Indians to make room for Dr. Buchman's ancestors who emigrated to America from Switzerland. It is odd that those Americans who are so fond of declaiming against 'Colonialism' never pause to reflect that the United States of America is the most successful example in history of triumphant colonialism. The Indians are governing India but the Red Indians are in the Reservations.

M.R.A. is egalitarian in that it not only admits the rich and the poor, the aristocrat and the proletarian, the learned and the unlearned to its fellowship, but also to its platform, and bored though I have often been by the puerilities uttered in public, I fully appreciate the fact that if none but accomplished speakers were encouraged to testify in public there might be some ground for the charge of snobbery so often levelled against M.R.A.

The proportion of speeches at Caux to which I listened with attention was about as high as the proportion of sermons from which I have derived great profit. Many of those who spoke at these Assemblies had made a name for themselves in the world, and would have been listened to with attention whatever the audience they were addressing. Of the daily bulletins issued at Caux I appear to have kept very few, but of the half a dozen or so that I did keep, the report of speeches delivered on 23rd July 1955 is fairly representative. I was in Caux at the time, but instead of trusting to my memory I prefer to quote from the bulletins for that particular day.

Dr. Buchman, who was in the chair, opened with an important and timely definition of the relation of M.R.A. to the Church. He said: 'M.R.A. is not another Church. It is a gateway to the Church . . . We have men here from the Church who come to guide you of the Church into the way of Truth and help you check your guidance and be prepared to face any obstacles. We are not the Church. We are just a gateway.'

Monsieur Jean de Lavallée, consultant engineer and descendant of the family of Joan of Arc, said: 'I met M.R.A. in a prisoner-of-war camp in Germany in 1944. I was deeply grateful to be able to greet Frank Buchman at Le Havre when he arrived in France recently. I shared with him my vision to enlist 500 Catholic laymen. But that I now see was not the vision of Jeanne d'Arc. She thought of whole nations. So I had to rethink my estimate of what was actually necessary at this time of crisis. When one starts a war one does not hesitate to throw into combat twenty, thirty, forty millions. To destroy countries, cities or human lives one always finds enough, and for this fight we also have to find the thousands of men that are necessary.'

The wartime Chief of Staff to General De Lattre de Tassigny, General J. Touzet du Vigier, said: 'I found it difficult to go to Germany for the first time. A German miner said to me, "France is our hope." This man felt Communism was the danger, and he did not see anything but Moral Re-Armament to save him and his country. I, as a French General of a Tank Division who fought bitterly in the last war, became his friend. He was a former Communist, a miner and a German. This is the way to rebuild Europe for it cannot be done solely on economic and social plans.

Mr. Ludwig Kroll, German Federal Member of Parliament, said that he was intending to be in Caux for a month. 'I have seen,' he said, 'what it means to be committed to a world force for world revolution.' He outlined the growth of a new understanding in Europe, particularly between France and Germany. M. Claudius Petit, Cabinet Minister in six post-war French Governments, had spoken with Dr. Oberländer, German Federal Minister for Refugees, in Bonn before the curtain at the performance of *The Man with the Key*. He had said 'M.R.A. enables us— France and Germany—to be united for a common ideology in service to the world.'

The speech from the Caux platform which made the deepest impression on me was delivered by a Dutchman, the chairman of the Victoria Biscuit Factory in Holland. I am afraid that the printed record of what he said will not produce the same effect on the reader, for it was his personality and his shattering sincerity which captured the audience. Still, I will quote the verbatim report of Mr. Charles Redele's speech in the hope that it will help the reader to understand the influence of M.R.A. on men's lives.

When I had my first guidance I had to apologise to my competitor. I said to myself, I want to live these four standards and I want to listen to God, but this is the only thing I can't do. Give me a few other things to do. And every morning I got the same name of this competitor of mine. After three weeks I decided to say sorry. I said, 'I will say to this wrong fellow, "I am sorry", and that will be all.' Then God spoke to me: 'Why do you think he is a wrong fellow?'
Five years ago I had been dishonest with him and I had been jealous of him because for twelve years my father had been dead, and I thought I would be President of our Bakery Manufacturers' Association. And he was elected, and that is why I was so nasty to him all those years.
Then God told me I ought to go to him and tell all this. Again I had a very big struggle because I thought it is my sacred honour I have to give; because this competitor went all through Holland and told all my friends and officials that I was a second-class man, and everybody laughed at him and didn't believe him. And now I had to go to him and prove to him that he was right. That was the minute that God came into my life because before all this I didn't believe in God, because I was quite sure it was quite impossible for me to do this.
Then I got the feeling that it was a pleasure for me to go to

him. I told my co-director about it. He said, 'You are quite mad. You spoil your name and the name of the factory.' But I was so certain that I called him on the 'phone. He said, 'I am sorry, but I decided never to see you again.' The next week I telephoned again and got the same answer. The third week I telephoned again and he said, 'I am sorry, I am too busy. For the next four weeks I haven't got half-an-hour free.' I said, 'It doesn't matter, give me a little time in the fifth week.' So I went.

He received me then with a very closed face. I said, 'Be at ease, because I will tell you something that will interest you.' I asked his forgiveness for all the difficulties I had given him in the last six years and I told him quite clearly the dishonesty which I had against him and about my jealousy. And then he looked at me and said, 'What are you doing? What does it mean? How do you come to make this decision?' I told him I thought that God met me for the first time. Then he started to cry, and so did I, and so for a few minutes we were just sitting with each other and had to use our handkerchiefs.

Then he said, 'I am a very good Roman Catholic and I used not to work on Feast days and I tell you this is the biggest feast day in my life, and when you are gone, I am going home and will close my office and will not work today.' The next week I got a letter from him; 'I am quite sure we can fully use this spirit to build up a new spirit in our Manufacturers' Association.' And to finish I would like to tell you that a year ago his wife died, and three months afterwards I got a letter from him and he said that I knew how happily married he was, and he told me that he knew of nowhere he could find the answer for his sorrows, but he asked me if he could come and spend a day with me at my home with my wife, and together he spent a day in my home, and when he left he said, 'You have given me a force to go again to life and to come over my sorrows.' And that shows you how very very friendly we are together now.

VII

PRE-JUDGEMENTS

CRITICISMS of M.R.A. are of two kinds. There are the criticisms which are the product of prejudices, that is the pre-judgements of those who lack the necessary *Zetesis* to find out the facts, and there are the criticisms which are based on post-judgements, that is on judgements which are arrived at only after a careful examination of the evidence and after conscientious research. Conscientious research, however, takes time, and we are under no obligation to devote the necessary time to examine the claims of every new religious or political panacea for the ills of mankind.

I have, therefore, no quarrel with the man who, in effect, says, 'What little I know about M.R.A. does not appeal to me or encourage me to undertake the necessary research which alone would make my opinion on M.R.A. worth expressing. I therefore refrain from comment.' Such restraint is, however, unusual, for it is only a select minority of human beings who are restrained from passing hostile judgement on things which they dislike by the fact that they can't be bothered to find out the facts.

In the case of M.R.A. there are, I believe, a fair number of people whose position is much the same as that of a friend of mine who said, 'I admit that I'm prejudiced against M.R.A., and I'm not prepared to wade through the propaganda literature published by M.R.A. I don't know enough about them to check their claims, but I would like to read a book by an impartial and detached observer who was not trying to put anything across, either for or against M.R.A. Meanwhile I'm quite ready to admit that my own prejudices may be due to misconceptions.'

In this chapter I propose to discuss some of the more popular misconceptions of M.R.A.

(1) *M.R.A. Ignores Christ and Leads to Indifferentism*

I have already quoted Dr. Buchman's unequivocal disclaimer of any intention to found a new Church. 'M.R.A. is not another Church. It is a gateway to the Church.'

M.R.A. is neither a Church nor a Sect. It is a spiritual discipline which all men can practise irrespective of their particular creeds. Within the movement itself there are, as I shall explain in a later chapter, many different conceptions of guidance, but no Catholic could possibly quarrel with the basic principles on which all MRAs agree, that men should seek to ascertain and to act on the guidance of God, and should measure their own conduct by absolute standards of love, unselfishness, purity and honesty.

It is true that Christians in M.R.A. do not stress the beliefs which divide them from the non-Christians, but it is a fallacy to deduce from this avoidance of controversy within the fellowship of M.R.A. that the Christians regard the specifically Christian dogmas as of secondary importance. This is very far from being the case. It would be easy to fill this chapter with quotations from the speeches which Dr. Buchman has made at Caux and elsewhere in which his devotion to Christ is affirmed and re-affirmed. The leadership of the movement is profoundly Christian, and the Christians in the movement are always ready to help any non-Christian who is beginning to realise that Theism is not enough. MRAs are convinced that those who seek God's guidance will be guided into all truth. They have faith in our Lord's promise recorded by St. John (14:26): 'But the Comforter, which is the Holy Ghost, whom the Father will send in my name, he shall teach you all things.'

St. Francis Xavier on his sea journey to India gave scandal to one or two rather straight-laced Catholics on board because he consorted on terms of such cordial and familiar friendship with certain loose-living soldiers. 'I will go in by their door,' said the Saint, 'that they may come out by mine.'

M.R.A. goes in by the door of the Muslim or the Jew or the Buddhist, in order that they may come out by the Christian door. As indeed some of them do. I remember a conversation with a Buddhist in M.R.A. Buddha did not believe in a personal God, and he founded not only a religion but an ethical system which has some affinities with modern Positivism. I put this point to the Buddhist in M.R.A.: 'How can you seek the guidance of a personal God if you don't believe in a personal God?'

'Since I followed the M.R.A. way of life,' she replied, 'I have come to believe in a personal God and I do not think that I am really entitled to describe myself as a Buddhist any longer.'

M.R.A., precisely because its terms of reference are not explicitly Christian, can soften the prejudices of those Asiatics and Africans against a religion which too many of them tend to identify with the hated ascendancy of the West. Even in countries which are nominally Christian there are many millions who are spiritually even less mature than the Israelites whom Moses led out of Egypt, and are as unprepared for the full Christian revelation as were the pre-Christian Israelites. Be that as it may, I believe that for many, M.R.A. may prove to be 'the Gateway to the Church' in a more exact sense than Dr. Buchman intended.

The policy of refusing to identify M.R.A. with Christianity in order to attract non-Christians the more readily into the Christian sphere of influence necessarily involves the use of some description of their message which has no obvious religious undertones. Hence the use of the ugly word 'ideology', ugly because of its unpleasant associations. The original significance of this word did not disturb the MRA, for none of them so far as I could ascertain had ever had the curiosity to trace the word 'ideology' back to its first inventor. I write subject to correction, but my own researches lead me to the tentative conclusion that the word *idéologie* was first suggested by Destutt de Tracy to the *Institute de France* in 1798 to describe the origin and nature of ideas, by those who accepted Condillac's philosophy of mind. Condillac derived all knowledge from the senses. In other words, 'ideology' was the equivalent of the philosophy now known as materialism. In 1812 Napoleon rightly blamed the ideologists 'for the misfortunes through which our beautiful France has passed'.

Finally it is of interest to note that whereas M.R.A. has been criticised for failure to emphasise its Christian origins, Dr. Buchman has been given to understand that Rome can only continue to permit Catholics to co-operate with M.R.A. if M.R.A. concentrates on its social programme of good will, and avoids as far as possible explicit references to our Lord, lest Catholics who are present might be confused by interpretations of Christ's teaching which deviated from Catholic Christology.

(2) *'The Buchmanites are always telling people how successful they are'*

The words which I have quoted at the head of this section are taken from a letter written to me by a Catholic priest. I concede that the M.R.A. presentation is often unfortunate and suggests a complacency of which M.R.A. are not guilty. In effect, what they are always telling people is not how successful *they* are but how successful God is. God, so they argue, has the remedy for all the ills of this distracted planet. Listen to God, accept His guidance, change, and you will become a changer of men, and, through men, of the world.

I can see no essential difference between the enthusiasm with which MRAs recommend their spiritual discipline and the conviction with which the early Christians proclaimed the virtues of what a Greek theologian called 'the medicine of immortality'.

(3) *Apparent Complacency*

Again it is a question of presentation, and I am not surprised that many casual visitors to Caux have been irritated by the apparent complacency of those who talk so big about the Four Absolutes. I confess that I have sometimes felt that what was wanted was a Fifth Absolute, Humility; but as superficial acquaintance with the MRAs at Caux deepened into friendship, I became more and more convinced that the discipline of M.R.A. does in fact bear fruit in a very genuine humility.

Sir Harold Nicolson, in his fascinating book *Good Behaviour*, draws a comparison between the effect produced by the early Christians and 'the converts to Buchmanism'. He writes:

The prejudice against the Galileans was not due to their doctrine or their form of worship so much as to their bad manners. It was their attitude to the non-elect which irritated people, not their faith.

There was in the first place their exclusiveness; their habit of meeting together in private conclaves; the way they addressed each other as 'brother' or 'sister' when in no way related. In the second place they adopted a sanctimonious manner, a self-satisfied expression, and indicated in their gait the superiority of their morals. Even thus, in the early days, could the converts to Buchmanism be recognised by the manner in which they would prance along the Tottenham Court Road. . . .

The MRAs would, of course, be flattered by this comparison to the early Christians, and would accept it as exact on at least one point. Sir Harold's description of the effect produced by the early Christians is derived from the gross misrepresentations of those who hated them. *Mutatis mutandis*, the same is true of the caricature of 'the converts to Buchmanism prancing along Tottenham Court Road'.

Sir Harold seems to have had slight qualms about his urbane contempt for the early Christians, for he writes:

As a humanist and an apostate I may have been unfair to the early Church in the chapter that I have devoted to her manners. I am irritated by her pharisaism and iconoclasm: but I regard her ultimate teaching with respect.

And there are many who are irritated by the idiom of M.R.A. but who, none the less, regard with respect not only the basic teaching of M.R.A. but the lives inspired by that teaching.

(4) '*A suggestion of snobbishness about their policies*'

Once again I must *subpoena* the *advocatus diaboli*, Mr. Geoffrey Williamson. He writes:

There was a suggestion of snobbishness about their policies which hardly measured up to the repeated talk about 'inspired democracy'. I have already mentioned the way in which everyone was given a superlative 'build-up' whenever introductions were being effected, usually exaggerating their attainments, as in my own case, or laying particular emphasis upon titles or good family connections. 'He's the son of so-and-so', or 'His cousin is the Duke of so-and-so.' It was also manifest that it was the Buchmanites' unswerving policy to cultivate the wealthy and the influential, and to display less concern for the underdog. A small nucleus of ordinary folk, miners, steelworkers, shipyard hands, and others were included, to be sure, and some of them were put forward on the platform at every opportunity, but I noticed that the individuals selected in this respect were usually men in key positions in their industry, shop steward, union officials or people who might be expected to influence their fellow workers.

Mr. Williamson's account of his reception made me feel vaguely envious, for I find it difficult to recall a single occasion on which anybody referred to my own attainments when introducing me to their friends, but I do recall Kit Prescott's malicious amusement when a Norwegian whom he invited to lunch to meet me asked me if I had ever skied, and I remember another MRA at Caux with whom I had some pleasant talks, and who later met me at Zermatt. He seemed faintly surprised to meet me among the mountains, and asked me if I was visiting Zermatt for the first time.

Certainly no effort was made to inform me of any social or other notables who were staying in Mountain House. I remember an attractive girl who waited on our table in the dining-room on more than one occasion. I asked her name and discovered she was the daughter of a duke, and that her brother was in Mountain House at the time, but the information was not volunteered, and though I must have spent some weeks under the same roof with this lady and her brother I never met them and do not even know the brother by sight. Whereas, if Mr. Williamson is to be believed, they would immediately have been produced as evidence of the kind of people who were attracted by M.R.A.

Like other civilised people, my friends at Caux took the trouble to tell me something about the background of the people whom they arranged that I should meet, but there was no 'superlative build up'. I may add that my wife, who spent some time with me at Caux, and who was critical of many aspects of M.R.A., was surprised that I think it necessary even to waste time refuting this charge of snobbery.

You will, I admit, find in M.R.A. publications the names

of prominent people who have joined M.R.A. travelling teams, or visited Caux, and it is right and proper that you should. The first line of attack on M.R.A. was to insist that the 'Buchmanites', as their enemies called them, were nonentities, adolescent cranks who lacked the intelligence or the experience to resist the cheap appeal of a wandering American revivalist. If the personnel of M.R.A. is relevant to this argument, as the enemies of M.R.A. seem to suppose, I cannot see why it should be regarded as permissible to make incorrect and damaging statements about that personnel, and improper and snobbish to give the facts. And the facts are that M.R.A. makes its recruits from every social class and from every race. If I were to offer no evidence for this statement I should lay myself open to a charge frequently, and with some justice, brought against M.R.A., of making exaggerated claims without offering adequate evidence. If, on the other hand, I offer evidence I shall run the risk of Mr. Williamson's displeasure. That risk I am prepared to take. Here are some names in a typical M.R.A. team, a team which toured South Africa:

Rear-Admiral Sir Edward Cochrane, K.B.E., R.N. (Ret.).
Rev. George Daneel, Minister of the Dutch Reformed Church, South Africa, a well-known Springbok rugby player.
Miss Rosa Grabe, who first heard of Moral Re-Armament at a Communist University in East Germany and escaped to the West to attend the World Assembly at Caux, Switzerland.
The Marquis of Graham and his sister, Lady Fiona Graham.
Captain Loudon Hamilton, M.C.
Lady Hardinge of Penshurst.
Mr. Bremer Hofmeyr, a former Rhodes Scholar at Oxford.
Colonel the Hon. Malise Hore-Ruthven, C.M.G., D.S.O., formerly commanding The Black Watch.
Mr. Paul Kurowski, a Ruhr miner, for twenty-five years an official in the German Communist Party.
Mr. Ivan Menzies, for thirty years in the Gilbert and Sullivan operas with the D'Oyley Carte Opera Company.
Sir Roy Pinsent, Bart.
Mr. E. G. Sarsfield-Hall, C.M.G., former Provincial Governor in the Sudan.

E

At Interlaken I was far less surprised to meet an occasional aristocrat among the converts to the Oxford Group than a characteristic specimen of my old college, Bernard Hallward, D.S.O., for he seemed to me the sort of person who had been conditioned by the intellectual climate of Balliol to reject any presentation of religious truths which did not conform to accepted canons of taste. I was no less startled when I heard that Canon Streeter, Provost of Queen's, had been converted to the practice of M.R.A., for he was a scholar for whom the Oxford idiom was second nature. His presence at Oxford Group House Parties did indeed produce much the same distressing effect in Oxford circles as the secession of Tertullian to those second-century Enthusiasts, the Montanists, provoked among Christians seventeen centuries ago.

There is one quality with which we must credit converts to M.R.A.—great moral courage—for it is far easier to defy hatred than derision. Only philistines and uncivilised fanatics are unaware of the debt which European culture owes to the Church of Dante and Chaucer, Van Eyck and Michelangelo, and even the architects of a secularist utopia who hate the Church as the enemy of all that they call progress, would not deny the Church's contribution to culture. Admittedly the household which the Catholic convert enters is not only that of St. Francis and the builders of the great cathedrals but also of Alexander Borgia and Torquemada, yet even they are impressive in their own unappealing fashion, and certainly less dissuasive to the products of Balliol than the popular conception or misconception of Dr. Buchman. There was, at least, nothing *risible* about the Spanish Inquisition, whereas the very terminology of M.R.A., 'guidance', 'sharing', 'quiet times', etc., invites caricature. 'Then too,' as Maisie Ward wrote in 1937, 'the movement has in various ways laid itself open to ridicule. Rose Macaulay, though with less than her usual subtlety, had made it seem particularly absurd in her novel, *Going Abroad.*'

Those who maintain that M.R.A. is tainted by snobbery might at least reflect that its enemies have no more potent ally than fashion. M.R.A. is as unfashionable as primitive Christianity. Every convert to it must begin by winning a

victory over his own brand of snobbery, be this social, academic
or aesthetic, and must be prepared to defy a barrage of sneers
and derision which is a far more exacting test of courage than
anger and hatred. They were brave men, those architects of
the Oxford Group. I salute them, though I am not of their
company.

Mr. Williamson, on the other hand, swims happily with the
tide. It is fashionable in this age of fake egalitarianism to criticise M.R.A. for trying to 'change', as they would put it, or to
'cultivate', as Mr. Williamson puts it, 'the wealthy and the
influential'. I have been long enough at Caux to have discovered that Dr. Buchman is no apostle to the genteel. What
impresses one at Caux is that the MRAs care, and care tremendously, for people irrespective of their class or race, and
dedicate their lives to the task of making people happy—
through 'change', as change is understood at Caux. Of course,
the MRAs realise that the conversion of some natural leaders
is more important for the cause which they have at heart than
the conversion of an obscure individual with no following.
But this is not snobbery, it is common sense. Was it snobbish
of Wiseman to make a special effort to convert Newman?

Mr. Steven Runciman contributes to the jubilee addresses
of the Historical Association an entertaining defence of historian's snobbery.

> Narrative historians [he writes] are often accused nowadays of
> snobbery. They tell us of the lives of the great and powerful and
> neglect that hero of modern times the 'common man'. Is that
> snobbery wrong? There have always been certain men and
> women in such a position in life that their actions, their whims,
> their physical and moral weaknesses, have affected the destinies
> of whole nations. There was in Western Asia in the Middle Ages
> a spiritually minded and astute—if deplorable—sect called the
> Assassins. When the Old Man of the mountains sent out his
> Assassins to perform their professional tasks he did not tell them
> to assassinate the common man. He knew that to achieve poli-
> tical aims one must be snobbish in one's assassinations. Whether
> we like it or no, we must pay due attention to the great.

Mr. Williamson's attack is symptomatic, for as Mr. Evelyn
Waugh somewhere remarks, we are becoming as self-conscious

about class as our Victorian great-grandmothers were about sex. The very word 'sin' is no longer used by those who conform to modern fashions and who would therefore be unperturbed by any criticism of their morals, but who would bitterly resent being accused of snobbery. Our Progressives would all be so much happier if only they would frankly admit that original snobbery is as ineradicable as original sin. Indeed, snobbery was *the* original sin. Eve was bribed by the serpent with the tempting promise of social promotion to the most exclusive of societies. 'Ye shall be as gods' said the serpent, and Eve promptly fell, the proto-martyr of snobbery.

A snob is, of course, a man who won't meet me, and a bounder is a man whom I don't want to meet, and so it is not surprising that the complex created by the snobbery whose existence in ourselves we deny, so often finds expression in accusations of snobbery levelled against other people. Mr. Williamson, after criticising M.R.A. for informing him about the backgrounds of the people to whom he was introduced, nevertheless records this fact for the benefit of his readers: 'I had put on an old school tie which Dr. Martin was quick to notice, for we had both discovered at our previous meeting that we were old Merchant Taylors.'

Though snobbery is a universal failing, the influence of which can be detected at Caux as elsewhere, I have never in all my long and varied experience met a group so free from class feeling and class consciousness, or any society in which people of different races, different social backgrounds, and different religions mixed more naturally on terms of more genuine and unaffected friendship.

(5) *'It was self-evident that money was being expended with prodigal extravagance' (Williamson)*

Mr. Williamson continues, 'The catering at Caux was of a quality to match that in the best luxury hotels.' An overstatement. The food in the small dining-room is better than in the main dining-room, but it was of the standard, so far as *ingredients* are concerned, of a good Swiss hotel, not of a luxury hotel. I made notes of the menus. The normal dinner was soup, a meat course, and a sweet or fruit. On Fridays no meat was served. The quality of the meals depended less on the ingredients than on the artistry and conscientious care of the kitchen teams that plan and prepare them.

I must admit that my wife and I, when we first came, did feel that as everything at Caux had to be paid for by sacrificial giving, the food should have been plainer,[1] but we were partially convinced by her cousin, John Phillimore, who said, 'Our guests come from all over the world. Some of them have travelled from the Far East to see Caux. We can't offer them wine or cigars, or even cigarettes, so we have to take particular trouble over the food.'

The standard of meals served in the small dining-room, which is reserved for guests, was about the same as on guest nights in a Benedictine Abbey or at Campion Hall, Oxford, with the important difference that the guests at these Catholic houses would be offered wine and cigarettes. Now whereas guest nights are few and far between in an abbey, every night is necessarily a guest night at Caux, for there is no day on which Caux is not entertaining guests who have in many cases travelled thousands of miles to investigate the claims of M.R.A.

Nothing could be further from the truth than to assert that money is expended 'with prodigal extravagance'. The cost of administration at Caux is only 2.5 per cent of the total expenditure, a percentage comparable with that of religious orders which, like M.R.A., depend very largely on unsalaried services.

M.R.A. is often criticised because its London headquarters are in and around Berkeley Square. There are many active MRAs who live and work in the East End, but a movement which does not confine its activities to any one class and which attaches importance to influencing men in key positions *must* be accessible.

There is another reason for a conveniently situated headquarters. There is a constant stream of people who have come into contact with M.R.A. who pass through London, and who arrive at all hours of the day and night. Many of them know

---

[1] It has become far plainer. I am told that the Swiss who financed the purchase of the hotel were convinced that all those who had been living for years on wartime rations required fattening up.

very little English, and all of them are grateful for the human interest and unfailing kindness of the MRAs who meet them on arrival, arrange for their hospitality either in the head-quarters or in the homes of M.R.A. sympathisers or elsewhere, and keep in touch with them during their stay. Of all the M.R.A. activities there are few which are of equal importance.

The Communists fully understand the importance of getting into touch with Africans and Asiatics on their way through London, and they make a special effort to deflect any Africans on their way to Caux. There have been cases where not only drink but women have been provided with the aim of recapturing Africans who had come under M.R.A. influence.

It is obvious that the work of M.R.A. in London needs some centrally situated headquarters. Some of the houses were bought during the blitz when property values in London fell sharply. None of them could be bought today for less than three or four times the prices originally paid. If the M.R.A. workers were scattered all over London, living in small homes or boarding houses, and paying bus and train fares into the headquarters, the cost per person would undoubtedly be far higher than it is. So far from their West End address having been an extravagance it has proved to be an economy.

(6) *Public Confessions*

Intimate confessions have never been encouraged in public, and on the few occasions on which an enthusiastic convert has been indiscreet, Dr. Buchman, if he was leading the meeting, promptly silenced him. It has, however, happened that a less firm leader has not applied the closure quickly enough, and such rare indiscretions are the only basis for the widespread belief, which of course those who dislike M.R.A. have done their best to foster, that M.R.A. encourages the more un-savoury type of public confession.

I did not, [writes Maisie Ward] in the eight or nine meetings which I attended, hear a single instance of the sort of indiscretion which I had been led to suppose marked Group Meetings. Most of the 'sharing' I heard seemed psychologically sound and very practical. It consisted more of telling what had been the result of asking for God's guidance and trying to follow it than of dwelling on the 'changed' person's previous state. It was in fact more of a confession of God's goodness than of man's weakness, and as such definitely stimulating.

(7) *Leakage*

Maisie Ward quotes a Catholic student of the movement who had collected evidence from various Catholics. 'All these witnesses are agreed that apparently immense results have a way of dwindling with startling rapidity.' Almost as startling perhaps as the dwindling of that 'very great multitude' who accompanied Christ into Jerusalem on Palm Sunday singing 'Hosannah to the son of David', but who ten days later were numbered among those 'who cried out the more "Let him be crucified" ', or among those who raised no protest when the crowd demanded that Barabbas should be released instead of Christ. I have often wondered whether Palm Sunday was not intended as a warning to all evangelists, clerical or lay, not to count too much on the constancy of converts.

I am told by M.R.A. that there is far less leakage today than in the 'thirties when Maisie Ward was writing. M.R.A. attributes this difference to the fact that in the early days of the movement there was no fully established team to follow up the work of an M.R.A. mission. The leakage among full-time workers is negligible.

But of course the real test of success is not how many people fall away but how many stay the course. A mission is worth while if only ten per cent of those who are converted from secularism to the Christian way of life, do not relapse.

(8) '*M.R.A. revels in all the brash slogans, yet refuses to translate them into practicabilities*'

The quotation is taken from *Moral Re-Armament. A Study of the Movement prepared by the Social and Industrial Council of the Church Assembly.*

Though I agree with some of the criticisms in this Church Assembly Committee's Report, I find it difficult to believe that those who compiled it have grasped the basic premise of M.R.A. Nobody in M.R.A. is such a fool as to believe that what this report calls 'pious platitudes', and what I would prefer to call the basic principles of M.R.A., are all that is necessary to solve political and industrial problems. Dr. Buchman, for instance, does not assume that there is no need for those who prepare the excellent meals at Caux to 'translate into practicalities' the M.R.A. principle that 'There is enough for the world's need and not enough for the world's greed.' Everybody at Caux knows very well that guidance is not the 'opium of the people', that guidance has to be followed up, and that sustained thinking and intelligent planning are essential whether the object be to produce good meals for hundreds of hungry people, or to solve a problem of social relations in industry.

What M.R.A. does maintain is that those who invoke God's guidance will think and plan to better purpose than those who do not, another example of what the Report would call a 'pious platitude'. It is certainly no new idea to any Christian that he should pray for God's guidance. The idea indeed is implicit in many of the great hymns, such as *Veni Sancte Spiritus*. One of the Oxford Group, to whom Maisie Ward quoted from the Litany of the Holy Name the invocation, 'From the Neglect of Thy Holy Inspirations, Lord Jesus deliver us,' was surprised to discover this M.R.A. conception in a Catholic litany.

I shall in due course criticize the M.R.A. theory of guidance, but for the moment I am concerned to expose a common misconception, as an example of which I might quote the comment of a friend of mine when a big strike was threatened. 'Now's the chance for M.R.A. to show what they're worth. Let them send one of their teams down to the strikers and work out a solution.' But it is not the function of M.R.A., *as a group*, to produce an official M.R.A. solution for a particular industrial crisis. It is, on the contrary, the conviction of all MRAs that if representatives of the management and the workers could be induced to begin the day with a quiet time and share their guidance, they would have far more chance of arriving at an equitable solution than those who rely on purely secular methods.

Whether this belief of theirs is justified is, of course, another matter, but for the moment I am only concerned to dissipate a fog of misconception so that MRAs can be criticised for what they do believe and not for what they don't.

(9) *H. W. ('Bunny') Austin's War Record*

Let me begin by quoting from an article in *Everybody's Weekly* (4th May 1946) from the pen of Rear-Admiral Sir Edward Cochrane, K.B.E., a war-time commodore of convoys.

One of the greatest figures in British sport has been condemned without fair trial by prejudiced publicists and a mis-informed public. His name is H. W. ('Bunny') Austin, the tennis player who helped Britain to win and hold the Davis Cup for four years.

. . . . .

Some people ask, 'How did Bunny Austin, an Englishman, come to be in America during the war?' He was invited there in the spring of 1939 by some of the representative leaders of the American nation, and received by President Roosevelt at the White House. He addressed a vast audience at Madison Square Garden, New York, and another of 30,000 people packed into the Hollywood Bowl at California, while over 10,000 more had to be turned away.

At that time America was like a sleepy giant, unaware of the full danger which threatened democracy and intensely sensitive to any 'British propaganda' which some Americans felt might involve them in another European war.

Yet Austin's interpretation to the American people of the best ideals Britain stood for was so effective that he was gladly received in state after state. The *San Francisco News* wrote: 'If this is British propaganda, let's have not less of it but more of it.'

Bunny Austin returned to Britain just two weeks before the war broke out. The winter of 1939 was the winter of the 'phoney war'. America became cynical about another 'Imperialist' war. At the end of 1939 Austin was once more urgently invited to America by those who saw the danger in which all democracy stood.

The British Foreign Office, the Ministry of Information and the Ministry of Labour were consulted. All agreed that Austin should go.

Later, Austin with other British nationals consulted whether they should return home or continue their work in the United States. The British consular authorities, acting on instructions from the British Embassy, advised them to stay on in America.

Some people have made it their business to spread the tale that Austin is a pacifist. It is not true. He has recently come out of the fighting forces after two and a half years' service.

He is in his fortieth year, and served exactly as every other soldier of his status and age group did under United States Selective Service regulations. . . .

In America, Austin and the M.R.A. workers went to work to draft a handbook of industrial and national team work, a simple straightforward ideology in everyman's language. It was called *You Can Defend America*. A million copies of it were sold in the United States.

General John J. Pershing, the only living man to bear the title of General of the Armies of the United States and leader of the American Expeditionary Force in World War I, wrote the foreword. The United States War Department described this handbook, written by Austin and his friends, as 'probably the finest statement of this country's philosophy of national defence which has yet been written'.

At the request of Service chiefs, State governors and Civic authorities, Austin and his friends moved through twenty of the most highly industrialised states of America. William Green and Philip Murray, the heads of the two great American trade union systems, as well as the big employers of labour, supported them in their efforts to reinforce the sound elements of American Labour in their battle against the anti-democratic cells and groups who were striving to slow down production and manoeuvre themselves into positions of control. . . .

Immediately the production curve began to rise. . . .

About this time, Senator [later President] Truman, feeling restless about America's industrial aid to the cause of freedom, was making a 35,000-mile trip across the country, inspecting countless factories and army installations. Back in Washington he was appointed chairman of the committee to investigate the war effort.

The success of the Senate committee launched Truman towards the Presidency. In the course of his investigations he came across the work of Austin and his friends. This is what he said of that work: 'I have given much time and thought to this matter, and have come to the clear conviction that these problems to which the Moral Re-Armament Programme is finding an effective solution are the most urgent in our whole production picture. Where others have stood back and criticised, they have rolled up their sleeves and gone to work. There is not a single industrial bottleneck which could not be solved in a matter of weeks if this crowd were given the green light to go full steam ahead.'

Recently, J. R. Steelman, Special Industrial Adviser to the White House and with the experience as conciliator of 80,000 war-time industrial disputes, publicly described Austin and his friends as 'the most effective single force for industrial conciliation at present operating in America'.

Even if I had not met Austin I should have no difficulty in believing that he was urged not only to return to the States but also to stay there, for I have the best of reasons for knowing what importance was attached by the authorities to making full use of Englishmen who could influence any section of American opinion.

In November 1940 I went to the States with the blessing of the Foreign Office for a lecture tour, the object of which was to win sympathy for my country. I received every help on my journey *to* America, but the authorities relapsed into evasive inaction when I tried to book a return passage, and it was not until I had invaded the office of the Naval Attaché and insisted on being given a berth on one of the six Naval cutters which had just been presented by the States to Great Britain, that a date was fixed for my return. A friend of mine, who was of military age, was being urged by the authorities to stay on in America in connection with propaganda. He consulted me, and I told him that he had his own reputation to consider and that I thought he ought to return, which he did, as indeed Austin would have been well advised to do had he been *primarily* interested in his own good name. I am, however, convinced that he was of far more use to England by staying in America than by returning home. There were many much younger men in England in reserved occupations doing far less valuable work.

One thing is certain. When Austin joined M.R.A. he sacrificed a brilliant future. He is not only an able man, who could have succeeded without the adventitious glamour of his tennis reputation, but he was also one of the idols of England after helping England to win and hold the Davis Cup for four years. He sacrificed financial security to work without a salary in a movement which had provoked widespread hatred and derision. He has given proof that he does not put self before service, proof which should convince all those who are open to conviction that his decision to stay in America was wholly disinterested.

(10) *The Charge of Pacifism*

The suggestion that M.R.A. gave encouragement to pacifists is a slander as baseless as the charge that Dr. Buchman was pro-Nazi. The following account of a sitting of the Conscientious Objectors' Tribunal before Judge Maurice Drucquer is taken from the *Oxford Mail* of 28th May 1940:

> Mr. J. M. Robbins of 15 Norham Gardens, Oxford (who had previously pleaded conscientious objection to fighting) wrote to the Tribunal: 'Since I came before the Tribunal on 30th April (1940) I have reached the conclusion that my place is with my fellow-countrymen wherever I may be needed. I feel that my objection was largely prompted by personal fear and I was helped to recognise this as a result of some talks with friends of mine in the Oxford Group. . . . I am sorry I have wasted time and public money and I enclose my fare from Oxford to Reading and back. I now ask that my name shall be placed on the military register.'

Every decoration for gallantry from the V.C. downwards was won by individual MRAs. One of the most gallant of a gallant company was a skier, Geoffrey Appleyard, who won the Roberts of Kandahar and led a team to victory against a Norwegian team chosen from west coast skiers. A wonderful tribute to his memory, by an American ski-ing friend, was published in the *British Ski Year Book* for 1946. Appleyard joined the Commandos, won the D.S.O., M.C. and Bar before being killed in Sicily. In a letter home he described his own moment of decision,

> You know that grand hymn, 'Once to every man and nation comes the moment to decide'—well, that moment to decide has come to me and the day I left home and the night I spent in London I made the great decision that I shall never regret, I know—that of giving my life to Christ.
>
> I haven't necessarily joined the Oxford Group, although I believe that in time this will mean full identification with them. But I have decided that I have tried running my own life on my own principles and standards long enough, and not made

a very startling success of it. So now I am going to run my life on God's standards and in the way He wants me to run it and so try and do my bit in the remaking and moral re-armament of the world.

M.R.A. was not only represented in the regular fighting forces but also in Resistance Movements. One of the most famous converts to M.R.A. in Norway, Fredrik Ramm, was arrested by the Nazis, and released because there was no evidence against him. He then wrote, as Editor of the leading Oslo daily paper, *Morgenbladet*, a series of articles which have been described as 'the very spear-point of Norwegian resistance'. He knew what awaited him. He was re-arrested and was only released from the Nazis by death. 'When the truth is told', said the Norwegian Foreign Minister, 'Ramm will go down to history as one of Norway's greatest heroes.'

(11) *'I thank Heaven for Adolf Hitler'*

On 25th August, 1936, Dr. Buchman was interviewed on his arrival in New York by a reporter of the *New York World Telegram*, who quoted him as saying:

> I thank Heaven for a man like Adolf Hitler who built a front line of defence against the anti-Christ of Communism. My barber in London told me that Hitler saved all Europe from Communism. That's how he felt. Of course I don't condone everything the Nazis do. Anti-Semitism? Bad, naturally. I suppose Hitler sees a Karl Marx in every Jew. But think what it would mean to the world if Hitler surrendered to the control of God. Through such a man God could control a nation overnight and solve every last bewildering problem.

Note the date, 1936. The civilised world had sent their athletes to the Olympic Games in Berlin. Prominent people in our country accepted the hospitality of thugs like Goering, just as prominent people have, and will continue to accept the hospitality of Communist thugs in Soviet Russia. There was a school of thought which held that once Hitler felt secure the persecutions, of which at the time very little was known, would cease, and that there was nothing to be gained by attacking him. Dr. Buchman himself was still hoping to change influential Nazis.

None the less, Dr. Buchman's remarks were unfortunate. Dr. Buchman was and is a great Christian leader, and he should not have publicly thanked Heaven for a man who had already inaugurated his persecution of the Jews, and those who claim to be the apostles of 'inspired democracy' should not imply that a dictatorship might be a good thing, provided that the dictator is God-guided.

Many critics of M.R.A. would be at least partially disarmed by an occasional admission that Dr. Buchman is not infallible. The attempt to maintain that in this case Dr. Buchman's remarks were well chosen is foolish, whereas any fair-minded critic would be mollified if the Group had more actively publicised their explanation, which might be summed up as follows: 'You have gone through Buchman's speeches and writing, and the writings of the Oxford Group with a comb of malice and the results of your gleanings are not impressive. In a public career of over thirty years this is the only remark of Buchman's which is embarrassing, and then only because it is tolerant of an interpretation which Buchman indignantly disclaims. Is there any public man who has been under constant attack for year after year, and who has never said anything which he has later regretted? Nobody who has made the slightest effort to understand what Buchman in particular, and M.R.A. in general, hope to achieve, could fail to realise that M.R.A. has nothing in common with Nazism or Communism. As indeed the Nazis fully realised.'

The Gestapo report, *Die Oxfordgruppenbewegung*, was compiled in 1942 by the Head office of the Reich Security Department. On 29th December 1945 the following letter appeared in *The Times*:

> . . . The document, which, as its title page states, was prepared by the head office of the Reich Security Department, concerns Dr. Buchman and the Oxford Group. It denounces them for 'uncompromisingly taking up a frontal position against National Socialism' in that 'they encourage their members to place themselves fully beneath the Christian Cross and to oppose the cross of the swastika with the Cross of Christ, as the former seeks to destroy the Cross of Christ.' 'Frankly, the importance of the Group lies here,' the document continues. 'At the very moment

when we [the Nazi Party] are making efforts to suppress Christian conviction of sin, which appears to us the first step towards the enslavement of the Germans, a movement is emanating from the Anglo-Saxons, who are racially related to us, which regards just this consciousness of sin as a basis for change in national relationships.'[1]

(12) *Aberrations there must ever be*

A middle-aged lady button-holed me in the lounge and began to tell me how she had been changed. I assumed my St. Sebastian manner as arrow after arrow, pointed with boredom, pierced my reluctant mind. 'I have my own idea about M.R.A. which I'd like to tell you, I think you'd understand, but I fear that my friends in M.R.A. aren't ripe for it. I believe there have been three Dispensations. First God revealed Himself to the Jews. Then came the Dispensation of God the Son, and now with M.R.A. we are entering on the Third Dispensation, God the Holy Spirit. Don't you think there's something in this idea?' I had no time to tell her that she was just seventeen centuries too late if she hoped to patent that particular idea, for at that moment a friend rescued me.

However bored I might have been by the earlier part of our conversation I had been fascinated by the sudden reappearance at Caux of an ancient delusion, which reappears from time to time among Enthusiasts. Little though she knew it, the poor lady at Caux was borrowing the categories in which Tertullian thought of Montanus, for Tertullian identified the coming of the Holy Ghost not with Pentecost but with the appearance of Montanus. St. Jerome summed up the teaching of the Montanists not unfairly when he wrote, 'God having failed to save the world by the first two degrees [of His revelation] came down through the Holy Spirit into Montanus.'

Eleven centuries later Abbot Joachim, according to the Fraticelli, made a similar division into three epochs. In the seventeenth century, 'Madame Guyon,' writes Monsignor Knox, 'claims that those who followed *her* way of prayer were

[1] Signed, among others, by the Bishop of Lichfield, Lord Ammon and Sir Cyril Norwood, then President of St. John's College, Oxford.

martyrs of the Holy Spirit just as the old saints had been martyrs for Christ.' *'Le règne du Père et du Fils sera rétabli et consomme sur la terre par celui du Saint-Esprit.'* And once again the old delusion of the three Dispensations surfaces at Caux. *Usque recurret.* With this difference. There is at Caux a core of sanity which corrects the extravagances of the lunatic fringe. An MRA to whom I reported this strange conversation was at first incredulous, and then horrified. I suspect that the neo-Montanist had an uncomfortable few minutes with him because when we next met she gave me a sad, reproachful look.

The Oxford Movement, like the Oxford Group, had its lunatic fringe. As indeed none knew better than Newman:

> Aberrations there must ever be, whatever the doctrine is while the human heart is sensitive, capricious and wayward. A mixed multitude went out of Egypt with the Israelites. There will ever be a number of persons professing the opinions of a movement party[1] who talk loudly and strangely, do odd or fierce things, display themselves unnecessarily and disgust other people. . . . Such persons will be very apt to attach themselves to particular persons, to use particular names, to say things merely because others do, and to act in a party-spirited way.

And it is as true of the balanced and thoughtful MRAs as of Newman's closest associates, that 'they were not answerable for the intemperance of those who dishonoured a true doctrine, provided they protested, as they did against such intemperance', as indeed my friend protested against the neo-Montanist. The point is important because those who busy themselves building up a case against M.R.A. so often concentrate not on the balanced statements of the leaders, but on the *obiter dicta* of the lunatic fringe, and this is grossly unfair, for, to quote Newman once again, the Oxford Group, like Newman's Oxford Movement, are 'not answerable for the dust and din which attends any great moral movement. The truer doctrines are, the more liable they are to be perverted.'

---

[1] 'Movement party.' This is what Newman wrote. Those who have read the typescript have all suggested 'movement or party'.

VIII

POST-JUDGEMENTS

THERE are two points which I must make by way of preface to this chapter, a chapter in which I shall try to summarise some of my post-judgements on M.R.A., that is to say the criticisms which seem to me valid *after* doing my best to find out the facts.

Firstly I wish to remind those of my readers who are practising members of a Christian communion that it is, as I have already insisted, unfair to compare the worst in a religious movement of which one is not a member, with the best in one's own communion. There is no Christian communion which has not been compromised by the sins of its members, and it is because I do not believe that the claims of the Catholic Church have been invalidated by Alexander Borgia and Torquemada that I am ready to admit that none of the criticisms in this chapter refute the claim that M.R.A. is an instrument of which God is making use.

Secondly, I wish to emphasise the fact that I am recording my personal reactions, and am well aware that my taste is not a final criterion. The over-simplifications of M.R.A. pronouncements probably appeal to far more people than they repel.

(1) *'This morbid distrust of intellect'*

There is one factor which reappears in every new manifestation of Enthusiasm. 'Always you find,' writes Monsignor Knox, 'this morbid distrust of the intellect cropping up.'

'One can,' as a Catholic priest remarked to me at Caux, 'have too much philosophy, but one can also have too little. The pendulum is always swinging between over-emphasis on reason and distrust of the intellect.'

F

The late Professor A. N. Whitehead, F.R.S., that distinguished mathematical philosopher, though an agnostic, paid a notable tribute to mediaeval theology.

> The Middle Ages [he wrote] formed one long training of the intellect of Europe in the sense of order. . . . It needs but a sentence to point out how the habit of definite, exact thought was implanted in the European mind by the long domination of scholastic logic and scholastic divinity. The habit remained after the philosophy had been repudiated, the priceless habit of looking for an exact point, and of sticking to it when found. . . . The greatest contribution of mediaevalism to the formation of the scientific movement was the inexpungeable belief that every detailed occurrence could be correlated with its antecedents in a perfectly definite manner, exemplifying general principles.

What one misses in most M.R.A. pronouncements is 'definite, exact thought'. The Middle Ages, as Whitehead insisted, was 'an epoch of orderly thought, rationalist through and through', and the temporary disrepute into which scholasticism fell was partially due to what Whitehead calls 'the rationalistic orgy of the Middle Ages'. Lutheranism was, in fact, a revolt against reason, and an appeal from reason to justification by faith, and it is not without significance that Dr. Buchman was ordained as a Lutheran Minister. But it was not only Luther who reacted against the rationalistic excesses of scholasticism in its decadence, against the philosophers who filled their pages with futile subtleties about catagorematices, and syncategorematices, and who wrote as if the only road to truth were by the well-tried milestones of *formaliter, materialiter, fundamentaliter,* and *eminenter.*

The author of *The Imitation of Christ* reminded his readers that it was more important to feel contrition than to know the definition thereof, a sentiment to which no Catholic could take exception. Bernard of Spires, on the other hand, whom Monsignor Knox considers to have been the first Quietist, was condemned for saying that an ignorant layman, when enlightened by prayer, can instruct better than the most learned of doctors. Though the germ of irrationalism was present in Bernard of Spires, and even perhaps in an occasional *obiter dictum* of the *Imitation,* as for instance *Quid curae nobis de generibus et speciebus?*[1] the balancing and corrective spirit in Catholicism not only corrected the excesses of rationalism, but also prevented the growth of irrationalism. Bernard of Spires, with his praise of the ignorant layman, represents a deviation from Catholic tradition which on this point, as on so many others, is represented by St. Teresa of Avilla's *buen letrado nunca me engano.* 'My opinion has always been,' wrote St. Teresa, 'that every Christian should try to consult some learned person, and the more learned the person the better.'

The ideal of the philosopher must be 'orderly, exact thought', but the revivalist, by his very nature, tends to over-simplification. Wesley, perhaps the greatest Englishman of the eighteenth century, was *un grand simplificateur,* the phrase that Brémond used about Bossuet. The over-simplifications of which critics of M.R.A. complain, are to some extent inevitable in an appeal directed not to philosophers but to ordinary people. 'In all pointed sentences,' Samuel Johnson remarked, 'some degree of accuracy must be sacrificed to conciseness', and Johnson's point could be supported by quotations not only from Dr. Buchman, but also from the Bible.

'Our intellectuals,' a French priest remarked to me, 'have no use for M.R.A. They think that it is all too *simpliste.*' A few, a very few intellectuals have joined M.R.A., and if their numbers were suddenly to increase it is probable that there would be less 'morbid distrust of the intellectual' at Caux. There is a suggestion of sour grapes in this attitude which again reminds one of earlier Enthusiasms. George Fox, for instance, valued, as Monsignor Knox drily observes, 'the inner light above all the learning which he lacked'. The Lollards again distrusted human learning as something 'carnal for which the children of light have no further use'.

'The intuition which comes from the direct *afflatus* of the Holy Spirit shall replace, for them, all their natural powers of discernment or of speculation.' It must be freely confessed that the sectaries who use this language with most confidence are not, as a rule, men remarkable in any case for intellectual gifts; there is a suggestion of sour grapes about the Lollard protest against the learned clerks of their day.[2]

[1] Why should we concern ourselves with genera or species?   [2] *Enthusiasm,* p. 221.

I must warn the reader that all generalisations about MRAs are subject to particular exceptions. It would, for instance, be incorrect to imply that all MRAs sweep aside as useless the rational defence of the Christian faith which we call Apologetics, but this is the general attitude. 'You can win an argument and lose your man', an M.R.A. once remarked to me with the air of a man who is saying something profound. But nothing could be less profound than this trite cliché. Would anybody dare to suggest that those great controversialists St. Paul, St. Augustine, St. Thomas Aquinas, and among Anglicans, those great apologists Paley, Lightfoot, Salmon, and in our own day C. S. Lewis, spent their time losing men? *They* did not dismiss the appeal to reason as a waste of time. One thing is certain, you don't win a man every time you lose an argument.

Garth Lean, an early Oxford convert to the Oxford Group, made a good point. 'We don't regard apologetics as useless, but we don't feel that's our job. We feel we can leave that to the specialists like you. Our job is not to prove that Christianity is true, but to change men and persuade them to listen to God.' Lean's attitude, however, is not typical. He is, like Francis Goulding, one of the few MRAs who are prepared to admit the value of an intellectual approach to religion, and to concede that intellectual difficulties have some importance. It is sin, so most MRAs feel, that keeps men from Christ, and *only* sin.

A Catholic priest at Caux was speaking of Dr. Morris Martin, who is very close to Dr. Buchman. Morris Martin was the youngest Doctor of Philosophy at Oxford, a brilliant scholar with a splendid academic future, had he not sacrificed everything for M.R.A. 'I have the feeling,' said the priest, 'that Martin is rather ashamed of his old interest in philosophy.' Next time I meet Morris Martin I am going to ask him whether he has been maligned, but be that as it may, I wonder whether an Oxford D.Phil. can elucidate one sentence in a broadcast by Dr. Buchman, which a group of trade unionists reproduced as a full-page advertisement in the *Daily Herald* (4th June 1956). 'The new alignment in the world is between the nations who think and the nations who will not think.'

What *does* this mean? I know that one of the more extravagant of M.R.A. over-simplifications is to contrast Soviet Russia united by a common ideology, with the divided West. Is then Russia one of 'the nations who think' . . . or, as Orwell would have said, only a nation which double-thinks? I was shown the script of this broadcast after attending Dr. Buchman's birthday party in London. I read the sentence I have quoted, to three or four MRAs who were in the hall, just before I left. 'What *does* it mean?' I asked plaintively. I remembered Whitehead . . . 'the priceless habit of looking for an exact point and of sticking to it when found . . .' I was quite prepared to stick to the precise point if only I could find it . . . 'What does it mean?' I asked again. The MRAs looked bewildered, sad and faintly shocked.

A friend of mine walked back with me from Berkeley Square, and admitted under pressure that this sentence did not mean much, but implied that I attached too much importance to what Whitehead called, 'definite, exact thought'. So I had often been told at Caux. How often have I been reminded that the Scribes and Pharisees rejected Christ, but that 'the common people heard Him gladly'. Oh, yes, the common people heard Him gladly, but not so gladly as Barabbas heard the common people when they demanded that Barabbas should be released and Christ crucified. . . .

If my friends want a quotation to refute me they had better quote St. Augustine. *Surgunt indocti et caelum rapiunt.* . . . 'The unlearned rise and take heaven by violence whereas we with all our learning wallow in flesh and blood.'[1]

'*La verité*,' said Renan, '*consiste dans les nuances*', but there are no nuances in M.R.A. 'The only class distinctions I recognise,' Dr. Buchman once said, 'are those between the changed and the unchanged.' All Enthusiasts begin by insisting that half a loaf is almost worse than no bread, and perhaps have some justification for their belief that there is more hope of converting the uncompromising enemy of the faith than those who, like Boswell, have 'resolved to maintain a decent system of mild Christianity', but some of them as they grow older are less exacting. 'When I was at Oxford,' wrote Wesley, 'I

[1] *Confessions* VIII 8.

was never afraid of any but the almost Christian', but in 1770 we find him writing to a friend: 'I have frequently observed that there are two very different ranks of Christians, both of whom may be in the favour of God, a higher and a lower rank. The latter avoid all known sin, do much good, use all the means of grace, and have little of the life of God in their souls, and are much conformed to the world . . .' but might, none the less, be 'in the favour of God'. Dr. Buchman, how-ever, will have none of this. The Prophet of the Absolutes is uninterested in the relatively good.

There is a certain connection between over-simplification and under-reading. I myself never heard any speaker on the Caux platform pay a tribute to the value of spiritual reading, but Francis Goulding tells me that such suggestions are made, but require to be worded rather carefully owing to the fact that the audience includes representatives of so many reli-gions. It is taken for granted that the Bible is read and studied, and there are many students of the Pauline Epistles and of lives of St. Francis. When I remarked to Francis Goulding that the Library should contain a representative collection of biographies of great Christians, he reacted with an enthu-siastic 'Hear! Hear!' which put me on the spot. If anybody cares to follow my example and present such books to the library they will be gratefully received.

There are some MRAs who are great readers of such litera-ture, but there are many more who would agree with the MRA who remarked to me that 'People come here not to read but to listen'. May be, but when I see MRAs consulting their little notebooks in which they write down the thoughts that come to them in their quiet times, I am always tempted to quote Samuel Johnson, 'Beware of a man who writes more than he reads.'

(2) *Moral Utopianism*

Authentic Christianity is neither optimistic nor pessimistic, for Christ offered to every individual the possibility of eternal beatitude or eternal damnation. The Church believes neither in inevitable progress nor in inevitable regress, but bases her realistic policy on the stubborn fact of original sin and its enduring influence. She entertains no utopian illusions as to the probability of any rapid and radical amelioration of human society. The Christian, indeed, is in much the same position as Virgil's oarsman who can just force his boat against the stream, but who, if he relaxes for one moment, will be swept headlong down the current.

> *non aliter, quam qui adverso vix flumine lembum*
> *remigiis subigit, si bracchia forte remisit,*
> *atque illum in praeceps prono rapit alveus amni* . . .

There are periods of advance when the rower gains against the stream, periods when the rower is carried downstream, and periods when all his efforts only suffice to keep level with some landmark on the bank.

There is a great passage in the *Apologia* in which Newman describes the effect on his mind of a world corrupted by original sin.

> Starting then with the being of a God (which as I have said is as certain to me as the certainty of my own existence, though when I try to put the grounds of that certainty into logical shape I find a difficulty in doing so in mood and figure to my satisfaction), I see a sight which fills me with unspeakable distress. The world seems simply to give the lie to that great truth, of which my whole being is so full; and the effect upon me is, in consequence, as a matter of necessity, as confusing as if it denied that I am in existence myself. If I looked into a mirror, and did not see my face, I should have the sort of feeling which actually comes upon me, when I look into this living, busy world, and see no reflection of its Creator. . . .
>
> To consider the world in its length and breadth . . . the corruptions, the dreary hopeless irreligion, that condition of the whole so fearfully yet so exactly described in the Apostle's words, 'Having no hope and without God in the world'—all this is a vision to dizzy and appal; and inflicts upon the mind the sense of a profound mystery, which is absolute beyond human solution. . . .
>
> And so I argue about the world; *if* there be a God, *since* there is a God, the human race is implicated in some terrible aboriginal calamity. It is out of joint with the purposes of its Creator. This is a fact, a fact as true as the fact of its existence; and thus the doctrine of what is theologically called original sin becomes to me

almost as certain as that the world exists, and as the existence of God.

Newman, though he hoped for the conversion of England, never wrote or spoke as if what he hoped and what he prayed for was probable. The contrast between the moral utopianism of the MRAs and the Catholic realism of Newman could be illustrated by comparing one of the most popular of the M.R.A. pamphlets, *The Rising Tide of Youth*, with the four lines in which Newman summed up his own reaction to the rising tide of secularism,

> He who spared Sodom for its righteous men
>   Still spares thee for thy ten
> But should vain tongues the Bride of Heaven deny
> He will not pass thee by.

To this the MRAs might well reply that our Lord spoke to His disciples of the Faith which could move mountains, and that nothing could have seemed more fantastically improbable than that a group of Galilean peasants should be the spear-head of a revolutionary movement which was destined to become the official religion of the Roman Empire, whose representative in Palestine had condemned their Master to death.

I have confined myself to a statement of fact that Christianity did become the official religion of the Roman Empire but I hesitate to write of the conversion of the Roman world to Christianity, because this is an ambiguous phrase. Do those who use it mean that the citizens of that Empire forthwith not only accepted Christianity as a creed, but began to practise Christianity as a code? That the general standards of morality were suddenly and miraculously raised? Alas, no. The convinced and apostolic minority, who not only accepted Christian belief but who also strove to achieve Christian behaviour, were outnumbered by the majority who accepted the religion of the state in much the same spirit that the majority of Russians accepted the ideology of the Marxist state after the revolution.

Christianity is not an alchemist's stone that magically and suddenly transforms human nature. It is a leaven, and a leaven which works slowly. None the less from the first appearance of Christianity this leaven began to influence the brutal world into which Christ was born. The Stoics disapproved of the cruel sports of the amphitheatre, but were complacently content to preen themselves as morally superior to those who derived pleasure from these barbarous spectacles, and the games went on until the monk Telemachus leapt into the arena and sealed with his blood a protest which there was no need to repeat, for the protest was instantaneously successful. The games stopped.

Most of the reforms which our modern secularists attribute to humanism were first introduced into Christian lands, and tardily adopted by such non-Christian countries as had come under the influence of Christian thought, and the men who passed on the torch of protest against cruelty and oppression claimed an apostolic succession derived from Christ. Even the reformers who had rejected Christianity, attacked abuses by the same irresistible argument, by the same reiterated appeal to a world leavened, but not revolutionised by Christ, to practise the principles for which Christ died, so that Christians were alternately incited to reform by the appeal of saints and goaded into reform by the taunts of sceptics.

The disappearance of slavery in Christian lands illustrates the working, the slow working of the Christian leaven. Christ did not formally condemn slavery, but He left His followers to discover that slavery was wholly incompatible with His spirit. Christians from the first had an uneasy conscience about their slaves, the first results of which were an improvement in the status of the slaves. Under Constantine and Justinian, a series of humane laws were passed which forbade the separation of slaves from their families, and which punished with death the violation of a slave woman. The tragic gradualness of the process whereby slavery disappeared in Christian lands is a striking example of the slow but irresistible influence of the Christian leaven. Christianity, as Chesterton somewhere says, 'was not merely an element, it was a climate; and in that climate a slave would not grow'.

The Christian leaven worked slowly, but the main point is that the leaven *did* work, that slaves *were* freed, that prisons *were* reformed, that factory acts *were* passed, and that all these crusades were led by devoted Christians supported by Christian men. And perhaps the most striking evidence of the importance of the Christian leaven is the fact that the horrors of the pagan world into which Christ was born have returned in apostate Russia, the first country of the West formally to reject Christianity. But even in Russia the Christian leaven is still at work. The Russian Government has repudiated Christ, but the second Person of the Trinity is nowhere a displaced person. 'Since Christ came into the world there has no longer been a world without Christ; He entered into it like a dye, the stain of which no amount of washing will remove, like a drop of God's blood which remains ineffaceably there.'[1] Yes, even the Communists have not eliminated that dye from Russia, but the Russian Church has been tragically weakened.

The Church is always beginning again, for ever picking up the dropped threads of missionary life. There was a time when it seemed as if Japan would become a Christian land, but all traces of Christianity were uprooted by one of the most savage persecutions in history. Nothing could seem more successful than the great Jesuit experiment in Paraguay, and that too came to nothing. The Christian missions made immense progress in China, and once again the work of centuries is threatened. Is there any reason to suppose that the pattern of past centuries will not be repeated? Gain and loss, loss and gain . . . losing on the swings what we gain on the roundabouts?

To this question most MRAs would reply, 'There is no reason why the pattern of centuries must necessarily be repeated.' To quote Dr. Buchman speaking in London in 1937, 'This is the revolution which will end revolution by changing human nature and remaking men and nations.'

Here are passages from those specially selected by the editors of *The Oxford Group and its work of Moral Re-Armament* from Dr. Buchman's speeches, and which therefore must be assumed correctly to interpret his message.

July 1935. *Oxford.* Could a quiet army of ordinary people, God-controlled, God-directed and God-illumined, be a force in a country, changing that community so that political leaders would

---

[1] Quoted by Ida Coudenhove in *The Burden of Belief.*

live in harmony and peace, so that parliaments would be God-guided and governments God-controlled?

This question, which clearly expects the answer Yes, is much the same as asking whether M.R.A. could not prove to be more effective than Christians during the first nineteen centuries of the Christian era, for politicians at peace with each other have hitherto been as rare as God-guided Parliaments.

August 1936. *London.* We can listen in every day. If we do, and if we obey what we hear, it is conceivable that together we will usher in the greatest revolution of all time, whereby the Cross of Christ will transform the world.

The 'greatest revolution of all time'? Greater than that which was led by the Apostles? Presumably not. Presumably what Dr. Buchman meant to imply was that the Christian revolution had been partially successful, and might now be wholly successful.

The same idea is put more bluntly by Peter Howard:

Buchman, the man of the future, [he writes] has taken the ideas of honesty, purity, unselfishness and love, of the guidance of God, and the possibility of change in human nature, which have existed in the world since men killed the carpenter's son, and given them in our time an international strategy and framework —Moral Re-Armament. He gave these ideas legs and they are on the march today.[1]

Peter Howard knows as well as I do that Christianity was on the march nineteen centuries before Dr. Buchman was born. The passage which I have quoted is characteristic of the kind of exaggeration which makes it so difficult for ordinary Christians to do full justice to Dr. Buchman and M.R.A.

(3) *The Boomerang Effect of Exaggerations*

It was said of a certain society, by a man who had abjured it, that its members scored by the exaggerations of their opponents. They were accused of murdering three men and a dog, and they triumphantly produced the dog alive. The enemies of M.R.A. triumphantly produce a dead dog and thus refute M.R.A.'s claim to have cured a dog and three

[1] *Ideas Have Legs,* p. 80.

men. Concentrating on the dog is the last resource of a controversialist with a bad case. The wise controversialist and the wise apologist is careful not to mention the dog. It is because I find the work of M.R.A. impressive that I am distressed by the exaggerations of Moral Utopianism. The trouble with exaggerations is that they have such a boomerang effect. Many people who are prejudiced against M.R.A. seize on some palpable exaggeration as an excuse for leaving the rest of the case unexamined.

A well-known barrister visited Caux for a day when I was there, and asked me to dine with him next evening at Montreux. A world mission of MRAs had been travelling through the East, and telegrams recording their success were being received daily at Caux. 'Somebody,' said my friend, 'read out a telegram from Egypt, and it seemed that Egypt had been captured for M.R.A., and then next morning I opened the papers and read the news from Cairo, a riot and people killed. What distresses me is that none of these people are encouraged to cultivate self-discipline in speech. They were handing out apologies last night to Africans because the British had exploited them. Why not devote some of their quiet time to the history of the British Empire in general, or of our rule in India, instead of shooting out undigested thoughts? Why all these ill-considered exaggerations? I suppose it's the American influence. Oh, for a little British understatement!'

I hope that my friends in M.R.A. will not sweep aside the criticism of my barrister friend as the reaction of the unchanged. He could have strengthened his case by quoting the following extracts from Peter Howard's description of the effects of the World Assembly at Mackinac in June 1951,[1] '*Those were twelve days that echoed round the world. . . . For at Mackinac a new type of man was moulded, a man governed by a fresh range of motives and of aims. . . .*" MRAs are always claiming to produce a new type of man. They have yet to prove that they can produce a rare but by no means new type of man, the authentic saint.

'*Statesmen began to act, no longer just to build up themselves or their own party, but to rebuild nations and the world. . . .*' Names, please. Which statesmen were thus influenced?

[1] *The World Rebuilt*, American Edition, p. 23.

'*Industry began to live, at this new altitude Labour leaders saw that as world renaissance became the accepted aim of the workers, strikes and showdowns were reactionary methods of settling disputes. The class struggle became irrelevant as men of every class were willing to change. Communists learned the secret of changing capitalists, and capitalists becoming honest about themselves began to change the Communists.*'

All this as the result of the Assembly of June 1951. Five years have passed since this world-shaking World Assembly. Has industry 'lived at this new altitude'? Has 'the world renaissance become the accepted aim of the workers'? Has the 'class struggle become irrelevant'? Claims made in the past can be checked, but it is less easy to discover whether the blank cheques which M.R.A. draws on the future will be honoured.

It would be easy to find out from neutral observers in California whether the following statement about Peter Howard's play, *The Vanishing Island*, is correct. '*The Vanishing Island* was launched in triumph on the west coast of America. It drew an overwhelming response from the mass of the people.' Less easy is it to prove or disprove, Ole Olsen's prediction that 'the songs in this show will be heard on all the juke boxes of America',[1] and quite impossible to discuss the comment of an unnamed admirer of the play. 'This is the genius of St. Francis, to make the theatre again good box office—and a herald of sanctity for the nations.'

As I bring this chapter to an end I am struck once again by the contrast between the reality and infelicitous propaganda of M.R.A. Peter Howard is a man of genuine humility, of which one is so conscious that when he tells one that what is good in his plays comes from God, and what is bad from himself, one knows that he is not talking for effect but expressing a sincere conviction. Furthermore I know from our many conversations that he has the profoundest respect for the Catholic Church, and a genuine reverence for her saints. Why, then, can he not take a little more trouble to express what he believes? Why write so carelessly as to leave the reader in doubt as to whether he is ready to dismiss as unimportant nineteen centuries of Christian history, and whether he really means to suggest that God had to wait for Dr. Buchman to 'give

[1] *An Idea to Win the World*, pp. 19, 20, 22.

legs' to the 'ideas of honesty, purity, unselfishness and love'?
I admit that over confident predictions and exaggerated
claims are no monopoly of MRAs. Many Catholics, for instance, greatly exaggerated the probable effect of Newman's
conversion. Finally, let me say that exaggerations can be
either positive or negative, and the positive exaggerations in
M.R.A.'s propaganda are venial compared to the negative
exaggerations which attempt to sweep aside as negligible the
very real achievements of this world-wide movement.

IX

'GUIDANCE'

It is, however, irrational to seek the guidance of
heaven about matters which the gods permit men
to decide for themselves, as for instance whether it
is better to engage an experienced or an inexperi-
enced coachman to drive my carriage. XENOPHON:
Memorabilia.

D R. BUCHMAN has summed up as follows his doctrine of
guidance. 'Accurate adequate information can come
from the mind of God to the minds of men who are
willing to take their orders from Him.' '*Can* come.' Agreed.
There are many examples both in the Old and in the New
Testament of information which was both accurate and adequate for the immediate purposes, reaching the minds of
particular men from the mind of God. But it is one thing to
admit the principle of direct inspiration in exceptional circumstances, and quite another matter to assume that such
inspiration is normally to be counted on. Now the words
which I have quoted from Dr. Buchman are tolerant of two
interpretations, the first of which every Christian must accept,
and the second of which most Christians would reject.

There are great differences of opinion among the MRAs on
guidance, differences which range from a view of guidance
which, as a Swiss Jesuit, Father Seiler, remarked to me, a
Catholic could accept, to the more extreme and sillier varia-
tions of 'telephone guidance'. As, for instance, a remark made
to me by an MRA who was motoring through Europe: 'My
guidance is to collect my letters. I did not know how long I'd
be here and I gave a *poste restante* address in the valley.' I felt
tempted to reply that as I had run out of postage stamps my
guidance was to go the post office and buy some more.

The unchanged are sometimes mildly irritated by 'My guidance is . . .', which seems to imply divine endorsement for what the unregenerate regard as a mere personal opinion. 'It is as if,' a priest remarked to me, 'they had a direct line to the Almighty.'

'I know what you mean,' I said. 'It is rather like talking to a spiritualist. A great friend of mine, a superb mountain artist, often introduces what he has to say with the words, "My Spirit guides assure me." My friend once had a long talk with King Albert of the Belgians whose comment on the conversation I have often felt inclined to quote at Caux, "You cannot argue with a man who gets his information direct from the other world." '

I can best illustrate the diverse conceptions of guidance by quoting specific examples which I recorded at the time in letters to my wife.

There was, for instance, a young man who told me that he was in love with a girl in M.R.A. and would not propose to her until he was quite sure that it was God's plan for him to do so. 'Of course,' I said, 'I believe that those who seek God's guidance and who dedicate their lives to His service will be guided in a general way, but some people seem to me to believe that you get far more detailed guidance than we ever claim for the Pope. Even when he is considering an *ex cathedra* pronouncement he uses all the human means at his disposal to come to a right conclusion. Our conception of Infallibility is much more that God won't allow him to say anything wrong than that God will put it into his head to say what is right. The relationship of the Holy Ghost to the Church might be compared to that of a flight instructor and his pupil in a machine with dual control. The pupil may make all sorts of minor mistakes, comparable to mistakes which many Popes have made in their ecclesiastical politics, but whatever erratic swerves the pupils may make, the instructor is always there to take over the controls, if that be necessary to prevent the plane crashing. I can understand your being ready to accept a strong and definite warning received in guidance against marrying this girl, but that is more like the instructor taking over the controls to prevent a crash, but if you're not prepared to propose to a girl who shares your ideals and your religion, and who seems eminently suitable, without waiting for positive guidance, you're in effect expecting detailed inspiration which seems to me a presumptuous expectation.'

'I do not expect to get detailed inspiration,' he replied, 'but what I do feel is that if one really tries to live by the Four Absolutes one will, as time passes, get more and more in touch with the mind of God, so that if I live for, say, ten years my guidance will be much closer to a hundred per cent divine guidance than it is today.'

I had many useful conversations at Caux with a full-time worker Basil Yates, an Oxford graduate and former Philosophy Don at Edinburgh University. We had tea together one day, and I instanced as a result of guidance that has proved to be misguidance, the adoption of the name Oxford Group. Somebody who was present gave the explanation which I had already been given, that the name was not their own invention, and that it was absurd to suggest that Dr. Buchman had adopted it for snobbish reasons. Not for snobbish reasons, I agree, but nobody would deny that Dr. Buchman has a genius for publicity, which is to his credit. If one has, as he believes he has, a medicine which can cure most of our maladies, it is his duty to give the maximum of publicity to his cure. In the early days the suggestion of some sort of link with Oxford may have appeared to him helpful, particularly abroad, but on balance the adoption of this name has proved very damaging. M.R.A. were bound to have enough trouble on their hands if they confined themselves to their legitimate objective, the campaign against sin, and it was a great mistake to risk a head-on collision not only with sin but also with Oxford. Oxford is a powerful freemasonry with great influence in all ramifications of the ruling classes, and one of the main reasons why Dr. Buchman has received great recognition in many countries such as Germany which awarded him their highest decoration, and France which gave him the Legion of Honour, and no recognition in England is the continuing hostility of Oxford.

Andrew Mackay heard me out and said, 'Well, I'll have to have guidance about this.' When he had left us, I asked Basil

G

Yates what precise process Mackay contemplated to get guidance as to whether M.R.A. had been misguided when they adopted the name Oxford Group. 'Well, I should think,' said Basil Yates, 'that he would begin by a prayer for guidance, and he would know that Christ was with him in that very room and ready to help him, and he would then write down the thoughts that came to him. Guidance is really no more than consecrated common sense.'

Next time we met, Basil Yates said, 'I would like to clarify what I said. My idea of guidance is that one should be conscious throughout the day of the presence of Christ, that one should feel that He is never far away, that one should be in touch with Him when in search of a decision. My guidance is just "consecrated common sense", but it would be wrong for me to conceal the rare occasions when it went beyond this, when I am sure that I got explicit and detailed guidance. When I first considered giving my life to M.R.A. I knew very well what would be the reactions of my colleagues whose good opinion I was anxious to retain. I had guidance to look up a particular text, and the text was "Be not ashamed".

'Here's another example. When I identified myself with the Oxford Group I realised that it would not be honest to preach M.R.A. in my lectures. I was not paid for that, but just before the first lecture of the term I had clear guidance to go to a certain drawer and take out a note book which I had used when I was eighteen. It contained an essay on the theory of punishment. It seemed to me crazy to begin the term reading an essay which I wrote before I went up to Oxford, but the guidance was exceptionally strong and I decided to follow it. I said to my class, "I'm going to read you an essay written when I was your age, and it will be an excellent exercise for you to pull it to pieces." Which they then proceeded to do with the utmost enthusiasm. It was a good exercise for them to find out the weak points in my argument, and naturally it was an exercise which amused them very much. As the result of all this my relations with my first class were excellent.'

Mrs. Basil Yates was an artist, working in stained glass, and when we met at lunch she talked with enthusiasm and with great knowledge of this beautiful craft. A few days later

I was lunching with her husband and the Dean of Copenhagen Cathedral, and realising that both the Yates possessed very sensitive aesthetic consciences I turned the conversation on to some of the things which had had such a violently dissuasive effect on me when I first met the movement. I had just been reading Maisie Ward's book on the Oxford Group in which she quotes an acrostic for prayer.

P owerful
R adiograms
A lways
Y ours

and also a slogan which seems to have been current in the 'thirties, 'A Spiritual Radiogram in every home', which is vulgar both in the technical and in the popular sense of the word; in the technical because it is designed to appeal to the vulgus, in the popular sense of the term because it debases the beauty of holiness to compare the operation of the Holy Spirit to a radiogram.

Yates maintained that what mattered was whether a particular phrase which might set his teeth and mine on edge, wins men for Christ. The Dean said, 'When you think of the reality of what happens when men get into touch with God, does it really matter very much whether some particular phrase or slogan irritates you?' Of course it does not matter *very* much, but it does matter.

If I find myself in a church which is a bad specimen of the worst period in architecture, the late nineteenth century, if the stained glass windows are insipid, and if the first thing I see is one of those sentimental mass-produced statues of the Sacred Heart, I can still say my prayers. The little red lamp burning before the sanctuary evokes the same response as the red lamp at Chartres, or as the lamp before which the Crusaders knelt at Acre. In relation to the tremendous reality to which that lamp draws attention, the aesthetic defects of the church do not matter much, but they matter a little. The Curé d'Ars was one of the holiest of saints, but his taste in ecclesiastical art was deplorable and nobody cared. But then the Curé d'Ars was a saint, and the world outside Caux does

not recognise in Dr. Buchman those marks of authentic sanctity which even non-Catholics recognised in the Curé d'Ars.
Moreover, there is always the memory of Chartres to remind
one that the ugly Catholic church is an exception rather than
the norm, but there is no such compensating glory to offset the
aesthetic dissuasions, which at least in the early days of the
movement repelled so many people who might have been
sympathetic.

No study of M.R.A. would be even relatively honest which
ignored the damage done, particularly in its earlier phases,
by the cheaper and less attractive of its slogans, but it would
be unfair to quote these slogans as if they were characteristic
of M.R.A. today. They are not. The presentation of M.R.A.
is incomparably more mature than it was when I first met
the movement in 1939. Moreover, even in those days there was
nothing in Dr. Buchman's manner which suggested a popular
revivalist's attempt to curry favour with an audience by play-
ing down to the lowest common denominator. The thing that
impressed me most about Dr. Buchman when we first met,
more than thirty years ago, was his dignity and reserve.

A few days after my conversation with Basil Yates and the
Dean of Copenhagen, I sat next to a lady at dinner who was
in the Foreign Office, Miss Metcalfe by name. I asked her
what her colleagues thought of M.R.A. 'Well, one of them
said to me,' she replied, ' "We all know that Dr. Buchman
did a marvellous job in Germany just after the war, and by
winning the confidence of the Germans, made things easier
all round, but we balance that against his pro-Nazism before
the war", whereas, of course . . .'

'I know . . .'

'Yes, I suppose it is unnecessary to tell you what nonsense
that is.' Of course it was unnecessary, but nonetheless I was
faintly irritated by a girl who sat next to me at dinner and
who explained that Dr. Buchman had foreseen the war because he had an ideology, and the politicians had nothing.
In the four great crises of our time neither Dr. Buchman nor
any member of the Oxford Group uttered a word in public
or wrote a line to help towards an understanding of the issues
involved. What is the use of an ideology which helps you to

foresee developments if you don't place your foreknowledge at the disposal of the well intentioned? And what is the use of talking about 'inspired democracy' if the inspired democrats keep their mouths resolutely shut on all the big issues which affect their country? I fully realise that M.R.A. could not reasonably be expected officially to pronounce on these issues, but the individual MRA had a duty to inform himself correctly and to do what he could correctly to inform his fellow citizens.

The first great crisis was the threat of Hitler. The Socialist policy was to cock snooks at Hitler, to abuse the Nazis and simultaneously to insist on unilateral disarmament. Even after Prague the Socialists voted against conscription. Incidentally, Peter Howard hints in one of his books that he was a collaborator in one of the most dishonest books ever written, *Guilty Men*, a book which attempted to make the Tories exclusively responsible for a policy of appeasement forced on the country by the pacifists. Howard, I believe, was pledged not to disclose his authorship, but a half-disclosure might have been followed by a half-hearted apology. ' "Sorry" is a magic little word.'

The second great crisis was the Spanish War. Just as in peace our effective choice at an election is seldom between a good government and a bad, but too often between a bad and a worse, so in this war the effective choice was between Communism and a watered-down Fascism. But few people now regret that Spain is not a satellite of Russia. George Orwell and John McGovern, M.P., a frequent visitor to Caux, were both violent opponents of Franco, but they both had personal experience of the ruthlessness with which the Communists liquidated rival leftists in Barcelona. I was sent out to Spain at Sir Arthur Bryant's suggestion to write a book which could be sent to every Conservative M.P. and political agent to keep them straight on this issue, and Neville Chamberlain said before his death that if it had not been for the Catholics, his Government would have found it difficult to resist the pressure to intervene against those who had risen to save Spain from Communism. The inspired democrats remained silent during the crisis.

The third great crisis was that of American intervention. Had the Nazis won in Europe and the Japanese in Asia, South America, where I spent some months during the war, would have fallen like an over-ripe plum. When I was in Santiago a German priest who had escaped from Germany preached to a congregation consisting in the main of Chileans with a German background. The persecution of the Church by Hitler was the theme of his sermon. In the course of the next week every member of that congregation who was susceptible to any kind of pressure, the boycott of his business for instance, or the possibility of unpleasantness for relations in Germany, was rung up on the telephone and warned not to attend that church on the following Sunday. And next Sunday the church was all but empty.

American intervention not only saved Europe. It saved America. The North American continent could not have survived indefinitely as an oasis of freedom in a world in which the Nazi-Japanese axis had conquered Europe, Asia and Africa and South America. It would be interesting to know whether any prominent American MRA helped those who were fighting the battle of intervention in America.

The fourth great crisis is the threat of Communism to the free world, and here at least M.R.A. is alert to the danger and has helped to alert others.

I put these points one morning when I was breakfasting with Basil Yates, who said 'As to the Spanish War, I just wasn't informed. Few of us were, but I do not at all agree that Buchman's silence on these issues was due to expediency. M.R.A. doesn't offer solutions to all problems. Our object is to change people so that they listen to God for His solution, not ours. We should do no good if we came to Africa with a ready-made solution for the terrible problems of this distracted continent.'

The more extreme conception of guidance, the expectation that accurate and definite information from the mind of God is something which we can hope for in all our difficulties, seems to me indistinguishable from the sin which theologians know as *tentatio Dei*. God gave us our minds to use and He gave us free will which implies the freedom to go wrong, that is, not only the freedom to do wrong but, if we are writers, the freedom to write badly. Peter Howard makes a point of the speed at which *The Vanishing Island* was written, and clearly believes that he wrote under guidance. I do not rule out the possibility of inspiration.

> Is there any writing man [asks Hilaire Belloc] with a true judgement of great things in writing, who does not doubt his own achievement, or is there any who when some particular piece of verse or rhetoric which he has written convinces him of its merit does not admit to his own soul that not he was the true author, but some force working through him?

Maybe, but even in the case of the inspired scriptures we are not encouraged to believe that the authors were the impassive instruments of the Holy Ghost. They too endured the drudgery of authorship, the search for the word or the phrase to convey their meaning. I do not imply that the M.R.A. authors believe that every line which they write is guided, but an over-riding belief in guidance seems to me the only explanation of the fact that so much that is careless finds its way into print, as for instance the following phrases from *The Vanishing Island*, all of which are again quoted in *An Idea to Win the World*. 'It's the secret the world is waiting.' One does not wait a secret, though one may wait for it. One does not 'Go down through milestones of history', but one may go past them.

> Remember that our readers
> Are all pinheads, and we turn
> Truth so that they may keep and feed us

does not seem to me to mean much. Howard does not write for pinheads, so why not take more trouble to exclude from his published work lyrics which even a pinhead could pull to pieces, as for instance,

> Deep in the heart of us, knowledge is breaking
> God in His glory the wisdom has shown
> Normal for all men to be world-remaking
> No class or race can achieve it alone;
> None can achieve it alone.

Normal for all, for colours and classes and races
United together, together an answer to find,
With a fire in our heart and a light in our faces,
Fulfilling the hunger and hope of mankind
The hunger and hope of mankind.

Hunger is not fulfilled. It is satisfied.

Howard is a gifted dramatist, but he should stick to prose, which is his medium.

The same carelessness robs so much of their propaganda of its effectiveness at least for the type of readers who expect a controversial case to be presented in accordance with some respect for the standards of scholarship. The achievements of M.R.A. are impressive, but the evidence for these is too often buried in page after page of undocumented assertion. Newspapers are quoted without an exact reference, and in some cases without even giving the name of the newspaper quoted, i.e. 'The editor of the leading Taiwan newspaper'. M.R.A. literature is full of tributes from unnamed admirers, i.e. 'One British diplomat said . . .'. 'A leading Trade Unionist told me . . .'; etc., etc. Obviously much that is said to MRAs cannot be quoted, but if the source of a tribute cannot be cited it is far better not to quote it at all. A record of M.R.A. achievement fully documented would be most impressive and worth compiling.

MRAs profess to despise controversy, but if their leading writers had ever submitted themselves to the discipline of controversy with an able opponent they would soon have acquired the habit of giving exact references. My friend the barrister was right when he complained of the lack of self-discipline in their writings. Life and letters; self-discipline is as important in the latter as in the former, and it is odd that those who are so self-disciplined in their lives are often so undisciplined in their letters.

I do not underestimate the popular success of Howard's books which have sold by the hundred thousand, and which have been an immense influence for good, but MRAs are very properly not content with a mere popular success. They want their plays and their best books to be taken seriously by the secular Press, and to be treated as important in the leading weekly papers. They are apt to attribute what some of them consider to be a conspiracy of silence to the influence of the 'unchanged', but first-class work cannot be ignored. Evelyn Waugh is a Catholic and a Tory who has been at no pains to conceal his contempt for the intellectuals of the Left, but his best work has been generously praised in *The New Statesman*, and an M.R.A. equivalent of Evelyn Waugh or Graham Greene could not be ignored.

I was present at the first performance of *The Vanishing Island* after the return of the World Mission to Caux. The comments after the play conformed to the customary pattern of uncritical praise, and my suggestion that some lyrics should be rewritten before the play was shown in London was coldly received. The London première was in May 1956. I read no critiques of the play in the Press, but I am told that there was a scathing comment on the lyrics in one of the evening papers. A friend of mine, Miss Philippa Hussey, to whom I gave a ticket, was much impressed by the acting and the music, but her spontaneous reaction (I had not divulged my own views) to the lyrics was the same as mine. Of this play Howard writes: 'It came naturally, easily and swiftly. It took just over two weeks to write, with an average of two and a half hours' work each day spent on it.'[1]

There is a little church at Campione with a memorial tablet to the masons of Milan Cathedral, and there is on the façade of the church an inscription which I commend to all M.R.A. playwrights and authors, an inscription which may be rendered thus:

By what remote parentage, by what silent preparations, by what vast agreements is nourished the eternal dream of art.

[1] *An Idea to Win the World*, p. 18.

X

SOME PEOPLE

MAISIE WARD, in her booklet, *The Oxford Groups*, compares an M.R.A. publication, *For Sinners Only*, with Father Martindale's *What are Saints?*: 'For Sinners Only* works like *What are Saints?* in the stuff of human nature, but how much narrower is its range. How exactly similar the various conversations described, how of one type the adventures of its heroes. *What are Saints?* is universal where the other book is sectional, it is of the widest and one might say wildest variety in its range of human experience.'

The comparison is not quite fair, for Father Martindale's saints are taken from nineteen centuries, whereas the Oxford Group was little more than ten years old when *For Sinners Only* appeared. Furthermore, Father Martindale is a writer of genius.

I agree that there is a certain sameness in the stories of conversion, but I was impressed by the immense variety of people one met at Caux. I discussed world problems with citizens of more than twenty-five different countries, and I picked up at Caux a great deal of information about Communist strategy and tactics. Long before Petrov had named certain Australians as agents for the Communists some of their names had been given me by an Australian at Caux.

Naturally many of the MRAs were anxious to describe their conversion; as a rule I listened to these confessions with interest, but I had sometimes to resist the temptation to tell them the story of the cynical Oratorian who remarked, 'What an interesting man Father Faber would be if only he could keep off religion.'

I remember an interesting Finn who lunched at our table one day. He had been an active Communist and spent some years in Moscow. 'Where shall I begin my story?' he asked. I suggested that he should begin just after he had apologised to his wife. He laughed a little uneasily, and my guess was correct, but I was spared his domestic troubles (which would have been of no interest to me) and was enchanted by his inside knowledge of the Soviet scene.

My Cicerone during my first visit to Caux was Christopher ('Kit') Prescott, and I was very sad to discover that he had not returned from Australia when I last visited Caux. Prescott had a good job in Cook's with excellent prospects, quite apart from the family connection between the Cooks and the Prescotts.

Here is his story:

'After I was changed my guidance was to leave Cook's and go up to Oxford and be ordained. I am one of a large family with no private means; I went to see the head of my college and told him I had no money but I was sure it would come along but could not guarantee it. . . . I got a legacy of £200 on the very day after I interviewed the head of my college. I wasn't expecting it. My sister with a bigger legacy was guided to help me, and then a lady whom I hardly knew wrote to say that she would guarantee the balance. Of course I gave up smoking and drink and lived as economically as possible. After taking my degree my guidance was that I should remain with the Group. I'm on the Committee of Management, so can draw no financial help in the way of expenses for journeys, but the money needed always turns up. If you were to go round among the full-timers here you would be staggered to find how little any of them have in the bank, a tenner here, less than that there.'

'How do the married ones with children manage?'

'Well, a schoolmaster who has been changed may educate one of the children, or somebody in M.R.A. who is working in the world, covenants to give them part of his income. The money turns up somehow. It's a rule that on our journeys we are responsible for finding our own fares unless somebody charters a plane and puts it at our disposal. I remember talking to Sir Roy Pinsent, a Birmingham lawyer, who was going to the Assembly at Mackinac. I told him that I was going and had booked my passage and was due to start in seven days, but the fare had not turned up yet. As I spoke, somebody came in and put an envelope in my hand. It was from a slight acquaintance and contained a cheque for the return fare. And so it goes on.'

I remember a few weeks before Prescott and his wife were guided to join the MRAs in Australia, asking him whether the fare had been found. 'Not yet,' said Prescott, 'but it will come along.' Which it did. There is something which is uncanny in this uncritical faith in guidance.

'Frank had been with us for some weeks,' said Prescott, 'in the industrial areas in England with the play, *The Forgotten Factor*, and when he left for Switzerland he just said, "Well, goodbye . . .", not a word as to how we should carry on. Once when he sent seven of the Group to South Africa, he saw them off at the docks, and took each of them aside. When the ship started one of them called the others together and said, "I think I should tell you that Frank said to me, 'You're responsible for this team.' " Whereupon they all burst out laughing because Frank had said exactly the same thing to all seven of them.

'When Frank was guided to send a team to Ceylon and India, he cheerfully announced that the conference would open on 11th October in Ceylon. Everybody told us that we could not get a passage either by sea or by air in time. Frank did not worry. About a week before we were due to go, a chartered plane was suddenly placed at our disposal by a group of Dutch and Danes who paid for it. Even so, for Frank to land in India with a big team and rely in the main on faith to finance them during their stay, took plenty of courage.'

Prescott, like all the other full-time workers, never seemed to get stale. My wife and I were impressed by his spontaneous laughter and chuckles at the first play he took us to, Howard's *The Real News*. The dialogue is excellent and there are many laughter-provoking lines, but if I had seen the play, as Prescott had done, at least twenty times, my laughter would not have been so spontaneous. It would seem, however, that the law of diminishing returns does not apply at Caux, for the MRAs troop in night after night to see plays they have seen dozens of times before, and apparently enjoy them as much the twentieth time as the first.

Prescott does not approve of visitors taking their eye off the ball. One evening he invited a very able Egyptian, a Doctor of Zurich University, to dine with us. The situation in Egypt was becoming critical, and I am afraid I switched the subject from his religious conversion to Egyptian politics. And for this I was very severely ticked off by Kit Prescott.

Leif Hovelsen's Story

Leif's father was a distinguished skier with a long record of successes at Holmenkollen. Lief was brought up as a Christian, but his religion meant little or nothing to him.

After Norway had been invaded, he joined the underground movement and was betrayed by another Norwegian who is now in prison.

'I was tortured,' said Leif, 'and on the list to be shot. I spent a month in solitary confinement. Though my religion meant very little to me, I had a great respect for our Lutheran minister who used to sing the words of the consecration, and perhaps that was why I remembered these words and sang them to myself in my cell, and little by little I began to feel that Christ was with me in the cell and that I was sharing in the sufferings of Christ.

'This long month ended, and I was taken out of my cell and could mix with other Norwegians. And because these men had no religion and were extreme left in politics, the vision of Christ which had helped me so much in the cell faded.

'One day a Norwegian who was to be shot—his name was Olav Wettersted—managed to pull himself up by the bars of his cell overlooking the court where the other Norwegians and I were awaiting the Roll Call. I knew him. We were friends, and suddenly he called out, "Leif, whatever happens to you, hold on to Christ!"

'I felt ashamed to reply, "I will, indeed," because I was surrounded by all those other Norwegians who had no religion, and I said nothing . . . nothing, and so I refused to my friend who was to be shot the only consolation which it was in my power to give him, the consolation of the words which would have let him know that I had pledged myself to Christ.

'I felt terrible . . . just like Peter after he had denied our Lord.

'Next day Olav was shot, and somehow his two friends and he managed to smuggle through to us a message, just a text from Romans, "Who shall separate us from the love of Christ?"

'It was in this camp that I met Dr. Skared, Professor of Ancient History at Oslo, who was of the Oxford Group. That was my first contact with M.R.A. When the Germans surrendered I was allowed to see in his cell the head of the Gestapo in Norway. The man was paralysed by fear. I told him that my mother and I would pray for him. The night before he was shot he received communion . . .

'I have been a full-time worker with M.R.A. ever since . . .'

Ex-Nazi

Herr Petersen was taken from his family as a young boy and educated by the Nazis in a school for the leaders of the future. He belonged to the élite of the younger generation. He fought through the war. A contemporary of his who had been through the same schooling took part in the liquidation of a large number of Jews. He came to Petersen in tears. 'All my training has done me no good,' he confessed. 'I hated killing those Jews. I am not worthy to be a Nazi.' He felt remorse because murder still awakened in him a feeling of remorse.

Petersen ended the war as an Officer Cadet. He remained an impenitent Nazi. Hitler had declared that if Germany lost the war this was only because Germany had proved herself unworthy of the great destiny that he had offered her. It was the duty of the young Germans, so Petersen felt, to accept the penance of defeat and make themselves worthy of the great destiny which would one day be theirs. He was imprisoned by the British but continued in prison the self-appointed mission of reinforcing the Nazi faith of his fellow prisoners.

It was at the end of 1946 that Petersen first came into contact with M.R.A. He was studying law in his father's office and he had been so much hurt by all that he had gone through that he did not want to get involved in any political party, much less with any religious movement. His plan was to bide his time until Nazism could revive. His friends and he were vague about the future, but they felt that war was inevitable, and that war would give them their chance.

'Deep down,' said Petersen, 'I was lonely and defeated, and that is why I kept to the Nazi faith as the one thing that I could hold on to. And then in Tübingen I met some fellows who were free and happy, and had clean eyes, which I hadn't, and I began to be curious as to what they had which I had not, and so when they invited me to a meeting of M.R.A. I went. I made it clear that I was still a Nazi and did not believe in God, but somehow they made me face up to the Four Standards, and I realised my need for forgiveness of sin, and the point of the Cross. I have given my life and my career, and what little money I still have to promote M.R.A. so as to fill the vacuum in many German hearts, for Nazism has been knocked out and nothing has taken its place.'

The 17th June Rising and After

I was in Berlin two days after the gallant but hopeless rising of 17th June 1953, and at Caux I met Herr Ballenthin, a young German who had ripped down the Soviet flag from the Brandenburger Tor, and in spite of fire from the Russian tanks, had returned to raise in its place the German flag. I only exchanged a few words with him, but I was impressed by his faith in M.R.A.

At a meeting in Caux on 5th October 1954, he said, 'I was convinced that the freeing of the East German population could only come through direct action. Here I have seen the absolute commitment in teamwork we need if we are to succeed in East Germany where so far our teamwork has failed. To be effective I commit myself to live this ideology so that we can give it to the East.'

At the same meeting Herr Karl Heinz Oehler, Chairman of the 17th June Committee formed in West Berlin after the rising, spoke. 'I believe that the spirit of Caux will have a very great part in bringing that unity to the West. We in the East Zone placed our trust in the West. When I escaped to the West I was disappointed at the disunity I found. Here at Caux I have found something which gives me fresh hope. In our battle to free our brothers in the East, we in the West must first unite ourselves. We cannot enjoy our freedom while millions are still enslaved. Freedom cannot be divided.'

A Rumanian Family

The Dachler family consists of a Rumanian engineer, his wife with a Swiss background but born in England, and British by nationality until she married, and two sons aged 15 and 17. After the Reds took control his wife, thanks to her British background, and their children, were allowed to leave Rumania for Switzerland, and a year later he obtained permission to leave. 'I was lucky. I still don't understand how I got away. . . . It was not by grovelling to the Russians, anyhow. Almost all those that did, have been shot. Within a few weeks 300,000 Rumanians were deported to Russia for forced labour.' Among them, I suppose, many of those wealthy Rumanians whom I used to meet in the bar of the Athene Palace during the first winter of the war. Incidentally one of the most entertaining books published during the war took its title from this famous hotel in Bucharest, *Athene Palace*.

'Many of the old corrupt gang of politicians,' my friend continued, 'took very good care to transfer small fortunes to Switzerland, and you may be sure that they did not wait for the Russians to enter Bucharest before decamping. They are now living on the fat of the land to the fury of thousands of Rumanian refugees who are living in the direst poverty.'

The Swiss Who Financed the Purchase of Mountain House

M.R.A. is indebted for Mountain House to three Swiss, Philippe Mottu, Robert Hahnloser, whose portrait hangs in the main hall, and Erich Peyer and their wives. The banks were on the point of selling the Palace Hotel, Caux, to a French group who were prepared to pay for the fittings, furniture, etc., after which the hotels might have been pulled down.

Ninety-five Swiss families decided to buy the hotel as a thank-offering for the fact that Switzerland had been spared the war. The three families principally involved, the Mottus, the Hahnlosers and the Peyers, began by giving a substantial slice of their fortunes. They were all well to do. They ended, as did three other families, by giving *everything*, *every* franc they possessed. It was not only Mountain House that they bought, but eight other buildings, hotels and chalets, at a total cost of three million Swiss francs, about £250,000 at the present rate of exchange.

Mottu was in the Swiss Foreign Office with every chance of a fine career. He resigned from the Foreign Office to devote his life to M.R.A. He had four children.

I raised a point that puzzled my wife. The MRAs at Caux all seem very well dressed.

'Nearly everything that the full-time workers wear,' said Mottu, 'is a gift. My coat was given me by one friend, my tie by another, my shirt by somebody I met a week ago, and so on.'

A young man who had been a prosperous banker in Geneva and who had given his *entire* fortune to M.R.A., remarked that there was a rich shirt maker in France who let any full-time worker go into his shop and take away a shirt without payment.

Mottu claimed that M.R.A. deserved some credit for the fact that Switzerland is comparatively free from strikes. And M.R.A. was largely responsible for a covenant drawn up between employers and workmen before the war. 'Of course, a lot of our influence could not be proved. It can be compared to the hidden part of the iceberg below water, but I'll tell you one thing. Whereas the churches pay taxes on gifts we do not, and I'll tell you why. Since we began to operate in Switzerland hundreds of people pay their tax honestly for the first time. The Government know this and to encourage us in our good work they let us off taxes on gifts, etc., which we should otherwise have to pay.'

'About strikes,' I said, 'I wonder what effect the M.R.A. slogan really has, "It's not who is right but what is right that matters." This seems to me to be saying the same thing in a different way. Every "What" has got to be argued by a "who", and if "what" is right, the "who" will be.'

'I agree,' said Peyer, 'but the odd thing is that it does work. I have a friend, an industrialist, and he had a labour dispute on his hands, and couldn't get any nearer an agreement. I'd told him about our methods and after a stormy session he turned to the representative of the workers and said, "Look here, some friends of mine at Caux are always insisting that in this kind of trouble one should try to find out not who is right, but what is right. Supposing we try their method and start off by being quiet for ten minutes and seeing if we can find out what is right." Which they did, and before they separated they had come to an agreement.'

A Heroine of the Dutch Resistance

A quiet middle-aged woman, this Dutch lady, who was awarded the Grand Cross of Merit of the Red Cross and, a little later, the highest order in Holland, the Order of Nassau. The citation mentioned her work for M.R.A.

Madame Charlotte Van Beuningen met M.R.A. before the war. 'During that terrible last winter of the occupation,' she said to me, 'I knew very well that many of the Dutch in the concentration camps were starving, and my guidance was to go in and insist on seeing the Commandant.' Clearly her chances of seeing him were very small, and her chance of never leaving the camp again were anything but small.

'My first guidance was, "I must not allow myself to feel fear. No man is wholly bad. Touch his heart." And when at last I was shown into his room my first question was whether he had any children. His face brightened and he began to talk about his son. And then I said to him, "Well, all these prisoners of yours are somebody's children." He said nothing at first, but then he gave me permission to send in food. I went round Holland collecting food, which was not easy, for the Dutch outside the camps were always near starvation. To prevent the guards stealing the food I had it made up into little sandwiches which were of no use to send back to their families in Germany, because they would have gone stale. I managed to supply over 15,000 prisoners with food. Then the Commandant was replaced.'

'And were you as successful with his successor?' I asked.

'I had the same guidance. Then he too was replaced and his successor would not see me because he knew that his predecessors had done what I asked them to do. But I went again and then at last he saw me. There were a thousand hostages in that camp, and the Commandant had orders either to shoot them or to take them back to Germany, but I persuaded him to hand them over to the Allies.'

A thousand lives saved. Certainly a tangible result to show for guidance.

Brief Encounters

I could write not one book but several if I had the space to record all the people who interested me at Caux. Instead, I am reduced to brief outline sketches. Here are a few jottings from my diary.

Lunched with the Romers. During the war he was in command of eleven tanks, and one morning during his quiet time before going into battle he had the clearest and most definite guidance that six tanks in a field were in danger. There was no apparent danger and the men in the field were happy making tea, but he interrupted the tea party, ordered the tanks to leave the field and felt extremely foolish. Suddenly six big shells landed where the tanks had been. From that moment on he was regarded as a mascot, and the men believed firmly that nothing would ever happen to the crew in his tank. And in point of fact nothing did.

Garth Lean arranged for me to lunch with two Swiss and their wives from Aargau. Both of them were tobacco manufacturers. Conscious of the anti-nicotine prejudice at Caux, they were wondering whether they should sell out and try some other line of business. They were much cheered by the story of Dr. Buchman's reply to an American manufacturer of beer who asked his advice: 'Make better beer.' The younger of these Swiss had had bad relations with his father. 'Was he a problem?' I asked. 'No, I was the problem,' and the rest of the story followed the M.R.A. pattern, apology to father, followed by reconciliation.

'Are your relations with your children difficult?' he asked hopefully. 'My relations with my eldest son Peter have always been all that I could desire, and more than I deserved. A most obliging boy. He captained the British Olympic Ski team, followed me into the Church, married exactly the wife I would have picked for him, and has done very well in his job.' My friend's face fell. He was a man with a marvellous cure, and here I was, obviously in need of treatment, pretending to be in robust health. To cheer him up I said, 'I have another son and a daughter, and I'm afraid my attitude to them when they were young could be summed up by quoting the traditional reference in the Queen's speech at the opening of Parliament: "My relations with Foreign Powers continue to be friendly." Friendly, but perhaps too detached.'

'And your younger children were hurt by this? and that created a division in your family?' said the young Swiss hopefully.

'Not at all. We're the best of friends.' After that he hadn't the heart to ask me how I got on with my wife.

An interesting breakfast with a young man of English descent from Rhodesia, and an American editor from Memphis, Tennessee, Meehan by name.

The Rhodesian, whose name I forgot to make a note of, said, 'In my quiet time this morning I had doubts about the wisdom of continuing to apologise to the Africans in public. This creates its own kind of superiority complex in relation to those who don't apologise, and encourages pride. I happen to be the sort of chap who does not mind apologising.'

Meehan: I agree. Emerson said, 'If you've injured a man, don't apologise, but offer him reparation. If you've been rude to him, go out of your way to be polite.' I'm an American, but I've a great admiration for the British, and I know that British Imperialism has done a power of good. And I did not like that play [*The Man with the Key*] the other night.

[The main characters in this play are diplomats specially selected to represent Britain, America, France and Russia at a top-level conference.]

Meehan: We have plenty of vulgarians in our country, God knows, but the kind of man whom we send to represent us at an important conference is never a vulgarian.

A. L.: I agree. I worked for your State Department in Germany and even in the lower ranks I never met anybody as crass as the American in the play. I've seen a great deal of your diplomatists in different countries, and I never met anybody in the least like the American in that play. The Frenchman was equally grotesque. The Englishman too was curiously unconvincing to anybody who knows the Foreign

Office world, but if you feel like that about the play why don't you tell them?

Meehan: Oh, well, they have their party line and don't like criticism.

The Rhodesian: I don't agree. I'm sure they would be interested.

Meehan: Well, I'm profoundly impressed, and until I have done a bit of life-changing myself I do not feel in a position to offer them my advice, but I'll tell you my reservations. First of all this guidance. Splendid if reinforced by the normal human method of arriving at a correct decision, but not otherwise. M.R.A. did a really wonderful job settling that Eastern Air Lines dispute. Nobody can dismiss that as unimportant, and afterwards some of the full-time workers came round to follow up, among them a nice young man who had been trained for journalism and threw up his first job before he really knew the way round. Now, if he had ever submitted to the discipline of holding down and learning a job, he'd be much more use to M.R.A. I don't like these young men throwing up their careers. They should make a success in their careers and use their position to influence people in favour of M.R.A.

One is always in danger of proving that other people's conclusions do not follow from one's own premises. I should be very sad if any of my grandsons threw up a good career to join M.R.A., but then I don't accept their premise that the choice is between world Communism or M.R.A. If I did, I'd think nothing more important than to work for M.R.A. If any of my grandsons, after a promising start in the world, joined a Religious Order, I would be proud and happy, but then I accept wholeheartedly the premise which leads to this conclusion.

Mrs. de Saint-Phalle of San Francisco was brought up in France, her mother being French, and was married to a Frenchman who became an American. Both of them were lapsed Catholics before they met M.R.A. Their two children left the Church as a result of their parents' indifference. Both came back. We talked about M.R.A. propaganda, and I agreed

that much of it was very effective, but that one missed in
their pronouncements the intangible quality of beauty. Many
of the sentiments expressed were unimpeachable, but they
were untouched by beauty.

Mrs. de Saint-Phalle: Perhaps that is deliberate. I know
many people who read the Gospels for their beauty and make
not the slightest attempt to change their lives to accord with
the teaching of the Gospels. Each century needs a new approach. We have to simplify the great truths. That is St.
Teresa's method, 'The Little Way'.

A. L.: Another point. Why isn't there a good library here
of spiritual reading? If these people read more they might not
be so repetitive when they try to describe their spiritual experiences.

Mrs. de Saint-Phalle: For many people reading is a form of
escape. What they need here is concentration on the need to
change. They want to force people to face themselves. No
distractions.

A. L.: What irritates me here is that instead of insisting
that they get wonderful results by their methods with many
people, they try to convince one that it is a universal method
which everybody must adopt. As a Catholic priest said to me,
'Many people have become saints without ever writing down
the results of their meditations.' I'm ready to agree that it
may be a good thing for three or four people to discuss their
lapses with each other, and I'm told that something like this
'sharing' has in fact been the practice in some Religious Orders,
but I do not see why Catholics who have the Sacrament of
Penance should be badgered to adopt this method. I was very
intimate with my brother Hugh, but when we were young we
never discussed our amorous adventures with each other. I get
terribly embarrassed when people start talking about their
more ignoble forms of sexual lapses. Nothing would induce
me to discuss my past except in the confessional, and that
wasn't much fun. I remember an eminent Catholic convert
coming down to see me after I was received. 'How did you
get on in your General Confession?' he asked. 'Oh, it consisted of a lot of questions, did I do this or that, followed by
a lot of "Yeses".' 'Where did you score your first "No"?'

asked my friend. I told him. 'Oh, I had to wait for murder for my first "No",' he replied. I remember a Protestant heckler who got up at the end of one of my lectures in Australia, and said, 'When you decided to join the Roman Church what was your approach to the Confessional?' 'Slow and reluctant,' I replied.

Mrs. de Saint-Phalle: I was brought up in the French tradition, where it is unheard of for such matters to be discussed, and I feel as you do about reticence, but we at Caux find that if people have really attained to Absolute Purity they can discuss these things among themselves without discomfort.

A. L.: You may be right. I remember a doctor telling me that whereas a prostitute, if told to take off her clothes for a medical examination, will often pretend to feel embarrassed, he remembered once being called in to examine a Reverend Mother who was ill, and this involved her being practically nude. She took off her clothes without the slightest fuss or embarrassment. Sex had been so eliminated from her life that even nudity was not remotely connected in her mind with sex.

It is only fair to add that in all the time that I was at Caux I was only twice embarrassed by a personal confession which was forced on me. Nothing of the kind is permitted on the public platforms. Sharing is always done by members of the same sex in all teams, and in such teams I am prepared to admit that the confession of a sexual lapse may be salutary.

Whereas the visitor to Caux is impressed by the excellent food, the teams in smaller centres often feel the pinch. Mrs. Beeman, whose husband was a Canadian Brigadier, worked with the team in Trieste. They were often short of food and just got down on their knees and prayed for it till it came along in money or in kind, and tided them over for a day or two. When the team was ready to go to Caux they had no money for the fares, and at the last moment a cheque arrived from Canada.

In 1939 I was convinced that M.R.A. could have no appeal to Latins, particularly to French or Italian Catholics. I felt that nobody who was born and bred in the Catholic culture could find M.R.A. anything but uncongenial. I was wrong. Count Malherbe, for instance, belongs to an old Normandy family. He was very active in the Resistance, and he was one of the leaders at Caux till the Church asked all Catholics to withdraw from positions of leadership. He could understand and appreciate my antipathy to the idiom of Caux because he had felt, and indeed in some ways still feels, as I do.

I was constantly meeting people at Caux whom I assumed had the same kind of detached and friendly interest in the movement that I have, people to whom its idiom must, so I felt, be as unattractive as it is to me. And then I would discover to my somewhat shocked surprise that they were fully committed as, for instance, the Baroness Flaghac, a member of a very ancient Portuguese family. Her great-grandfather was Chancellor to the last Emperor of Brazil, and she married a Frenchman. She is in the early fifties, still beautiful, and she speaks French with that exquisite artistry which is a delight to hear, no matter what is said.

'I met M.R.A. in Brazil,' she said, 'and got to know them very well. I was impressed by the courage with which they faced poverty. One day they told me that they had no money left. 'What will you do?' I asked. 'We shall pray and somehow the food will come to feed us for a day or two.' That evening somebody gave them a little money. They were often hungry, but they always got just enough.

'I met there some Negroes who had been changed. They told me how they had often made money by helping people smuggle in goods through the customs. But they had given all that up now that they were changed.'

The Baroness had at first been angry with the M.R.A. attitude to wine, but she had come to the conclusion that drunkenness was a terrible problem in France, and had given up wine.

It was this Baroness who gave a very valuable ring to finance the African play, *Freedom* (p. 48).

A Swiss family, the de Wattevilles, are represented in almost every European country. One of them raised a battalion to fight with us in India in the early nineteenth century. The

Baronne de Watteville belongs to the French branch of the family. She is not the kind of person who might be expected to like M.R.A.

'We are accused,' she said, 'of being anti-intellectual here. Well, in France we had all the intellectualism we could possibly want. And what is the result? Nothing. The only dynamic idea in France today is Communism. You know Howard's book *Ideas Have Legs*. Well, at the time of the French Revolution French ideas *had* legs. Our revolutionary armies crossed the Alps and the Pyrenees, but today French ideas are legless. Lots of clever talk . . . oh, yes, . . . too much.'

Mrs. Barrett, a granddaughter of Lloyd George, saw a lot of him in his last months. 'He was interested in M.R.A., and said that perhaps it was the solution. He knew then that the Treaty of Versailles was a bad peace, and perhaps he guessed that he had been unable to make a good peace because there was no unity in his own home.'

Over simplification once again. One of the finest peace treaties ever made was the Treaty of Vienna, which was fantastically generous to defeated France, a model of enlightened statesmanship. Its architects were Castlereagh who committed suicide shortly afterwards, Talleyrand, an apostate Catholic once a Bishop, with no morals, and Metternich who would certainly not have been regarded as changed had M.R.A. been active in his day.

Masid Movaghar was travelling round with the team as the personal representative of the Shah of Persia, rather striking evidence of the interest which M.R.A. is arousing in Asia.

'I used to own the Mehr newspapers,' he said, 'but I passed on the control to my nephew. I used to be anti-British, very much so, till I met this group, but now no more. I am a grandfather, and I come to Caux and these young men with whom I share my sins help me. They are the age of my grandchildren, but they take me kindly by the neck and they pull me out of the dirt.'

The stereotyped phrase may serve either as a substitute for

thought or as an unsuccessful attempt to express genuine
thinking. These alternative uses were illustrated in the course
of breakfast with one Indian and tea with another. At breakfast the conversation had turned on the Suez Canal, and an
Indian who was present remarked that of course his country
started with a bias against the Colonial Powers. 'Oh no, you
don't,' I said, 'you start with a bias in the favour of the only
great Imperialistic and Colonial Power in the modern world.
My country is no longer a Colonial Power, but nobody could
be politer than the Indians to the Imperialists who have sub-
jected country after country to a form of Colonialism infinitely
more oppressive than any Colonialisms of the past.' My Indian
friend looked thoughtful, and I hope that he may pause before he again refers to 'the Colonial Powers'.

I had tea with an Indian Labour Leader, Narasinga Rao.
He had worked underground against the British and been
arrested. He is now the Vice-President of the Indian National
Dockworkers' Federation. He met M.R.A. just before he
launched a big strike. He realised that his own personal
bitterness was a factor in the bad industrial relations, called
off the strike and apologised to the owners with the excellent
result that his object, payment for piece work, was achieved,
and the wages of the workers doubled. It was his own trade
union which had financed his journey to Caux.

'When I got here,' he said, 'I began to realise that I had
always thought myself a pretty good fellow, but that really I
had been an Imperialist husband and always wanted my own
way at home.' He then pulled out his little notebook and
began to read me the thoughts that had come to him in his
quiet time. I managed to take a copy because what he had
written illustrated my point. English is not his native language,
and he had therefore every excuse for employing stereotyped
phrases, and I quote what he said, knowing full well that it
will read very unimpressively. But I who heard the passionate
conviction with which he spoke knew that I was listening to
an attempt to convey a genuine religious experience.

'I may plan for my security, but there is no security in that
way. Such planning is foolish in a stormy world. If I repose
my trust in God He can look after me. The meaning of life

and the sum total of philosophies is there. Change, conquer yourself, and you can conquer the world. I feel the change and see a new life. God has a plan for my family too. I have hesitated all the while and today I found a new answer. There is no entanglement any more. I am a free man. From now on I want to live and do everything as in the presence of God.'

What could be more banal! But there was nothing banal in the profound religious experience which had transformed him.

Narasinga Rao is a Hindu. The Reverend H. Harawira is an Anglican priest. He is a Maori who was lent by the Church of England to the New Zealand Government to supervise welfare work among the Maoris. When it was suggested to him by MRAs in New Zealand that he should visit Caux he replied that he could not afford the fare. The fare was subscribed by M.R.A. supporters.

'At first everything at Caux got on my nerves. I did not like their methods. I was unpleasant to my room mate. When he suggested we should have a quiet time, I at first resisted, and then accepted because I was proud of my command of English, and felt that what I wrote down would be much better expressed than what he did. I had been a preacher, and had some success, and I did not want to face the fact that I had never changed anybody by my preaching. I met my room mate's good will by consistent unfriendliness. And then one day I woke up and realised how horribly I had behaved, and how my room mate had never shown by word or gesture the slightest irritation. He had never ceased to be kind and good tempered. And so one morning I said, "I'm really sorry for the way I've treated you," and he said, "Thank you. Now let us get on our knees and pray." That was the beginning. I have now resigned my Government position and am full-time with M.R.A.'

Mr. Harawira's case is typical of many of those who have been converted by the unfailing kindness of the MRAs and their resolute refusal to take offence. Like Mr. Harawira I have often felt contrite when I recall the discomfort I must so often have provoked by criticisms which, whether justified or unjustified, could not fail to irritate. My many friends in Caux have worked so hard with so little to show for their trouble so far as I am concerned. Indeed, I might well have placed on the title page of this book a line from Browning:

See how I come unchanged . . .

One morning I was joined at breakfast by a Nigerian and his wife, Mr. and Mrs. Chiwuzie, both of them school teachers. The day before I had met John Boyagis, a former captain of our ski team, and his wife Claudia who had also skied for Great Britain. I had met them by chance and they were surprised to find me at Caux. 'I thought,' said John, 'that this was something like Freemasonry which the Pope had condemned.' I suggested they should come and dine with me and make up their own minds, and it occurred to me that they would learn something of the impact of Caux on other races if they met the Chiwuzies who accordingly dined with us. There is a dignity and a naturalness about the finer type of African which is very impressive. They spoke quietly of the influence of M.R.A. on their lives and volunteered no criticism of the British until I asked them for their opinion of our own Civil Servants in Nigeria. 'Very honest and efficient, but until I met M.R.A. I had never been inside a white man's home.'

XI

A DISSUASION

Nobody who spends a few weeks at Caux can fail to be impressed by the heroic self-sacrifice of the full-time workers, and by the power of M.R.A. to evoke the devotion of men and women of different races, different social backgrounds and different intellectual attainments. My own respect and admiration for this great movement is, however, qualified by the post-judgements summarised in Chapter 8 and by another dissuasion which is the theme of the present chapter.

God created the good things of this world that they should be enjoyed, and it is normal for man to enjoy them. The pleasures of wine and of sex are legitimate pleasures which should be accepted with gratitude. The puritan may be defined as a man who condemns legitimate pleasures as sinful, in contrast to the ascetic who is prepared to sacrifice a legitimate pleasure in pursuit of a higher form of happiness. The priest, for instance, sacrifices the legitimate pleasures of sex as the price to be paid for the happiness of the vocation to which God has called him. But he does not condemn the pleasure of sex as sinful. If he did, he would be guilty of the heresy of puritanism.

This mischievous heresy reappears from century to century under different names. The Manichees condemned as sinful both the eating of meat and the drinking of wine. The mediaeval heretics, the Catharists, whom the mediaeval Inquisition was founded to suppress, condemned sex as sinful. Marriage was condoned but not approved, and the 'Perfecti' who did not marry were deemed to be the only genuine Cathari. The Muslims condemned wine and laid waste many provinces in the kingdom of art, those for instance which were concerned with the representation of the beauty of the human form.

The same desert fury which swept into fallen Constantinople and hacked to pieces the glorious Iconostasis of Santa Sophia, reappears in Calvinism which robbed so many mediaeval cathedrals of their great legacy of statues and stained glass.

MRAs walk a tight rope between asceticism and puritanism. In theory at least they do not condemn drinking or smoking. They leave each man free to follow his own guidance in the matter. A man is not necessarily a puritan because he abstains from wine, provided that he does not condemn explicitly or implicitly wine drinking as wrong. It is clearly a good thing for the full-time workers, who are living on the sacrificial giving of other people, not to smoke or to drink, but the pressure not only on full-time workers, but on MRAs in the world, to give up smoking and drinking is continuous and irresistible, for I have never met anybody associated with M.R.A. who either drinks or smokes. And sometimes the less prudent MRAs overstep the line which divides the ascetic from the puritan. In one of the M.R.A. publications the Reverend E. V. Asihene, Moderator of the Presbyterian Church of the Gold Coast, is quoted as saying in the course of an address to MRAs, 'You have stopped your smoking and drinking, gossiping and sex-driven life'; thus confusing in the same sentence what is sin (for this I take to be the implication of 'sex-driven life') and what is not sin. It is much as if one were to say, 'You have stopped eating unnecessarily good meals and committing adultery.'

One evening at dinner I sat next to a Dutch Baroness, whose name I forgot to record. She is the cousin of a famous skier, Gratia Schimmelpenninck. I said something to the effect that I do not like the M.R.A. attitude to wine, and she replied, 'Ah, that means that you're very fond of wine,' a typical reply. The MRA are uninterested in rational argument and admit only one explanation of a disagreement with M.R.A. principles—sin.

'What would you think,' I asked, 'if a barrister replied to the arguments of another barrister by remarking that his learned friend argued as he did because he was being paid a very high fee by his client?'

'I don't understand the point,' said the Baroness.

'Only this,' I replied. 'Arguments have to be met by arguments, not by a diagnosis of the motives of those who employ them. You realise this in the case of a barrister. Nobody asks or cares whether he believes in his client's case. He is there to put that case to the jury. Similarly, it is quite irrelevant to ask whether I am an intemperate drinker or not. My arguments would not be strengthened if I were a teetotaller or weakened if I were a dipsomaniac. Actually, if drink had been one of my problems I would have given it up . . .'

'Would you?' asked the Baroness.

'Yes, I say it with conviction. I used to smoke twenty to thirty cigarettes a day. In 1953 I decided never to smoke again. I have not smoked since. That entitles me to say that if I could not control my drinking I am convinced that I could give it up. I don't need it. I can go for days on end without a drink and not miss it. I have been here a fortnight and have only tasted wine once. I went down to Vevey for that Fête des Vignerons, incidentally the finest pageant that I have ever seen, and I drank three *décis* of white wine at a neighbouring tavern to propitiate Bacchus, and as an expiation for the water drinkers of Caux. It is as unreasonable to assert that nobody should drink anything but water because many people misuse God's gift of wine by drinking too much, as to assert, as did the Cathari, that all sex relations are wrong because the gift of sex is misused by fornicators and adulterers. Wine is part of European culture. It is quasi-sacramental.'

I remember so well my return to the Alps after the long war exile. The moment that I got out of the train I went straight to the station restaurant at Berne and ordered three *décis* of Fendant. A ritualistic drink. The keen wind of the glaciers, and the benediction of the snows, and the glory of youth among the mountains, all seemed bottled in that wine. So too an integral element in the magic of Italy is the bottle of Chianti which I order with my first dinner in that sacred land. And as I lift the wine to my lips,

> The years dissolve I am standing in that hour
> Of majesty Septembral and the power
> That swells the grapes when Autumn nights are still
> With silent stars on Orvieto hill.

The quotation is from the greatest poem that Belloc ever wrote, *In Praise of Wine*. Often at Caux I have recalled his attack on the water drinkers,

> For such as these in vain the Rhine has rolled
> Imperial centuries through the hills of gold
> For such as these the flashing Rhone shall rage
> In vain her lightenings through the Hermitage
> Or level browed Tourraine receive
> The tribute of her vintages at eve.

'Whenever a man,' writes Epictetus, 'drinks water only or submits to some ascetic practice, he takes every opportunity to talk about it to everybody. "I only drink water," "Why do you drink water? Is it just for the sake of drinking water? Man, if it be good for you to drink water only, don't say a word about it to the people who are annoyed by such persons." '

In justice to the MRAs it must be admitted that they seldom draw attention to their water-drinking habits, but the silent pressure of opinion is irresistible on those who join them, and occasionally the pressure becomes articulate even in the case of the unchanged. A friend of mine in M.R.A. once took me aside and said: 'You're well known, and some young man seeing you drink wine will say to himself, "If Arnold Lunn drinks wine, it's all right for me to." '

'A very proper deduction,' was my comment, 'but supposing I gave up drinking wine your hypothetical young man could still cite the supreme precedent and the divine example, our Lord.'

Our Lord did not merely drink wine. He turned water into wine and He turned wine into a sacrament. It is impossible to conceive of a less ambiguous indication that wine is one of the good things which God gave us, and which He intended that we should enjoy. The priestly vocation enjoins abstinence from the legitimate pleasures of sex; and there are circumstances in which a man must abstain from some of the legitimate pleasures of wine, but to imply that wine drinking in general is a sin is unchristian. I do not in the least resent the 'holier than thou' implications of the speeches at Caux addressed by the changed to the unchanged, for I know that the

MRAs are better men than I, but the holier-than-Christ attitude of those who imply, as the Reverend E. V. Asihene implied, that smoking and drinking can be compared to sins
against chastity, is an outrageous blasphemy.

I remember one night quoting to the MRA with whom I
was dining, the remark of an Irish priest who complained that
the movement was riddled with puritanism. An attractive girl
of twenty spoke up and said: 'That's just what I feel. Here
at Caux they are always going on at me about Absolute
Purity and I feel that they want me to give up poetry and
anything that might put impure thoughts into my mind,
Shakespeare, for instance, and they are always going on about
clothes being too *décolletée*, etc.'

Father Martindale was once discussing the translation of a
little pamphlet which he wrote, *The Difficult Commandment*, into
Portuguese. A Portuguese priest, laughing, said, 'In my country
perhaps the title should be altered to *The Impossible Commandment*.'
Chastity is, if not impossible, at least so difficult that the
Church has traditionally discouraged anything which though
not inherently sinful may aggravate the difficulties of avoiding sin or the occasions of sin. The Church is restrained by
prudence from condemning many border-line habits or practices, sanctioned by fashion, for the Church must always balance the chance of protecting those Catholics who heed her
warnings from unnecessary temptations, and driving Catholics
who sit very loosely to their obligations out of the Church.
The Church's attitude in all that relates to sex is much nearer
the austere M.R.A. attitude than might be supposed.

MRAs are as alive as the Church to the difficulties of the
difficult commandment, and are perhaps even stricter than
Catholics in general in condemning anything which aggra-
vates those difficulties. Whereas today an increasing number
of those who cannot accept the dogma of the Immaculate
Conception have no difficulty in subscribing to the dogma of
immaculate contraception, MRAs wholeheartedly agree with
Catholics in rejecting the latter doctrine. The world knows
little of the innumerable Catholics who, because their circumstances forbid them to increase their family, live lives of marital
celibacy, and such abstinence is also general among married

MRAs. Celibacy is not easy for a young priest. It is even more difficult for the married, particularly for those who, as is normal at Caux, share the same room. My criticisms of M.R.A. on points of detail are tempered by the fact that this spiritual discipline often flowers in a virtue which can fairly be described as heroic.

I remember one afternoon at an Assembly, when my mind was running on the contrasts between Rome and Caux, the chorus of young men and women began to sing. Kim Beazley, an Australian M.P. who was sitting beside me said, 'Look at those boys and girls. Can't you see a clean look in their eyes, the look which you only find in the eyes of those who have fought and won the battle against impurity.' I think he was right. The Mother of the Gracchi, when the Patrician lady from Rome was boasting of the grandeur of the Imperial city, pointed to her children and said, 'These are my jewels.' And these young people at Caux suggest a similar reply to the type of Catholic who dismisses M.R.A. with contempt.

XII

CONVERSATIONS AT CAUX

D URING my later visits I kept a careful record of the more interesting conversations at Caux. As I have commented in an earlier chapter on the habit of quoting anonymous tributes to M.R.A. I only omit the name of those whom I quote when I believe that this would be embarrassing to them. I do not think it fair to quote in a book an ill-considered remark which the speaker may regret.

A Mrs. Macbeth whom I met at Caux ran the usual line, that the British 'have not given their hearts to the Africans'.

A busy Civil Servant who works hard to bring order and hygiene, good government and education to a backward people can hardly be blamed if in his leisure hours he consorts with those who are congenial to him. To expect that he should give not only the best that he can in working hours to the Africans, but his heart to them outside working hours, is a counsel of perfection. We can respect those who follow this counsel of perfection without blaming those who do not. I have the greatest admiration for the MRAs who are showering affection on the Africans, as missionaries, Catholic and Protestant, have done before them and are deserving of all praise. That is their vocation. It is not necessarily the vocation of a Civil Servant, and it is as unfair to criticise a conscientious Civil Servant for not practising this particular counsel of perfection as to criticise Dr. Buchman because he does not imitate the Curé d'Ars by selling all the furniture in his rooms at Caux, Berkeley Square, Wellwood and Los Angeles, sleeping on bare boards, and living on a daily ration of a few potatoes, a little bread and some soup.

My constant nagging about the M.R.A. attitude to the British Empire had very little effect, but it did have a slight effect. After my talk with Lionel Jardine he made a speech at an Assembly from which the following is an extract:

> I belong to a family which has provided soldiers and admini-
> strators to the countries Britain has been governing for the last
> century or two. We are not ashamed of our family record, and
> I know that in this room there are others whose forebears have
> been in the highest position in those countries, and who look back
> on their forebears with pride and gratitude.

He added that he knew that other countries were critical of Britain.

> The fact is that the whole world would welcome a change in the
> British. I do not say that it is only the British that need changing,
> but we are talking about them. I say this because my decision
> is to start change in the only place in which I can start it, and
> that is in myself, in my family, and in my nation. As I am, so
> is my nation. I cannot expect my nation to be better than I am.

That is a moderate way of putting the case. If it were adopted as a model by other M.R.A. speakers who take the British for their theme, it would do something to reduce the legitimate prejudice against M.R.A. which is so prevalent to-day among people who resent the lack of charity and justice in the routine references to the British Empire on M.R.A. platforms.

It is a great illusion to suppose that it is necessary to attack the British record in order to 'win' the Africans. I'm far from convinced that it does not often have a dissuasive effect, even on the Africans. What *does* win the Africans is the warm affection with which they are received. I was present in the theatre when the World Mission returned, and I heard forty Africans singing their song, *Freedom*, which was written at Caux. The passion with which they sang was very moving. These MRAs have won their hearts as many missionaries but as few lay-men have done. They look after them in London, have them to their houses to stay and treat them in every way as equals, 'brothers for whom Christ died', to quote that great saint, Peter Claver, who loved and was loved by Negroes. M.R.A. has revolutionised the attitude of many key Africans who were attracted to Communism. Hundreds of Negroes have gone to Moscow and been trained as Communists. It is a toss up which way the continent goes, and M.R.A. is a powerful force on the side of sanity. I do not think that Moscow would waste their energy attacking M.R.A. on the radio and through their agents in the trade unions, if they did not regard M.R.A. as a serious obstacle to their plans.

It was surprising to find that Colonel and Mrs. Hore-Ruthven, their two daughters and Etonian son had enlisted in a movement founded by an American Lutheran. Colonel Hore-Ruthven is the brother of the late Lord Gowrie, who was Governor General of Australia, and he himself commanded a battalion of the Black Watch.

I remember once laying a friendly trap for the Hore-Ruthvens. A remark of Peter Howard's in the course of the World Mission was quoted in one of the daily bulletins. 'A man who does not change is a traitor to his country.' I asked the Hore-Ruthvens, with whom I was having tea, whether they thought that Churchill was a traitor to England. Naturally they were perplexed by my question, which struck them as idiotic.

'Of course not,' they replied.

'Do you consider that Churchill is changed as this word is understood at Caux?'

'I have a great respect for Churchill,' said the Colonel, 'but I would not describe him as changed.'

I then quoted Peter Howard's remark and asked the Colonel whether he thought that he himself had been a traitor to England before he had been changed. The Colonel, the best type of British officer, with a fine war record, began to try to suggest that in a manner of speaking he had perhaps been a traitor. This was too much for Mrs. Hore-Ruthven, for women are often more realistic than men, and she cut the conversation short.

I raised with Mrs. Hore-Ruthven the question of church attendance. The Catholics at Caux went to Mass on Sundays and there was also a good attendance at daily Mass. Not more than twenty-five per cent of the Protestants attended church on Sundays. Here are some of the explanations given.

'Most of us are regular in our attendance at home, but at Caux we're dreadfully busy. We get people for three or four days, and we just can't afford to drop the Sunday morning Assembly, and it is not easy to squeeze in church between the meeting at eight and the Assembly.'

'When I was first changed,' an MRA remarked to me, 'I was regular in attendance at church, but the parson was unchanged and uninspiring and I got nothing out of it.'

But one does not only go to church to get but to give. It is an act of allegiance and advertisement to the world that the creature owes certain duties to his Creator, of which keeping the Sabbath day holy is one. An inspiring priest is an extra which is very encouraging but which one has no right to demand as a condition for fulfilling one's obligations.

I often discussed M.R.A. with Lord and Lady Hardinge. Lord Hardinge, the son of a Viceroy of India, was King Edward VIII's secretary during the abdication crisis. Lady Hardinge has travelled more than once with an M.R.A. team, and would, I feel, be classified as changed. Lord Hardinge was detached, friendly but critical.

One night when I dined with the Hardinges and Garth Lean, Lord Hardinge started a discussion on guidance.

Lord Hardinge: I am prepared to admit the possibility of guidance in general, but I do not think we are meant to turn to God for detailed guidance. He gave us our brains to use.

Lady Hardinge: In my experience it is about details that people quarrel. About big difficulties they can usually be quite reasonable. I knew three women who helped with housekeeping, and quarrelled because they could not agree on the right way to make a bed. In their case guidance would only have meant a readiness to cross out their self-will and give in on a small point.

Garth Lean: Guidance means to me that I set aside an hour every morning in which I plan the day, I ask that God will guide me aright and I check what I believe to be His guidance with my friends. The final decisions are arrived at by prayer and consultation.

A. L.: I have just had a very interesting letter from a friend of mine with an acute intelligence, among the many points which she makes is that the explanations which M.R.A. offers seem to be reduced to the simplest terms, a common form which can only satisfy the readers of the more popular newspapers, and there is, she adds, a strong element of the ridiculous in the kind of over-simplification of complicated problems, particularly those which have occupied the minds of gifted men for centuries.

Lady Hardinge: I agree. It's a mistake to encourage people to think that there are simple solutions for everything and that a dose of M.R.A. will clear up every problem.

A. L.: In 1938 my wife and I went to an M.R.A. House Party at Interlaken, and what put us off was hearing a lot of young men talking as if the problems of war and peace could be solved if only the statesmen got down on their knees.

Lady Hardinge: Yes, I think we are vulnerable there.

A. L.: More recently I have read some M.R.A. bulletins with some very sniffy comparisons between Caux and Geneva. Supposing John McGovern, M.P., who is classified as changed, had been Prime Minister instead of Eden, does anybody really suppose that he'd have been more successful in handling the Russians at Geneva?

Garth Lean: Well, there is a short-term and a long-term view. None of us believe that the world would be radically changed for the better, even if our Prime Minister were changed. What we do feel is that if we do not get statesmen thinking on new lines things will go from bad to worse.

A. L.: What irritates me is the smug attitude you encourage among young people here who have had no experience of important jobs, and who make sniffy remarks about the statesmen who are dealing with these fantastically difficult problems, and who imply that M.R.A. knows all the answers.

Lord Hardinge: Exactly, and some of these statesmen aren't exactly fools, even if they are not changed. The trouble, of course, with M.R.A. is that there is no criticism here.

Garth Lean: You should hear us pulling each other to bits when we're planning policy.

Lord Hardinge: Perhaps, but I'm talking about the public assemblies. Nothing but back-slapping there. Why don't you invite some of the more intelligent outsiders who come here, to express their criticisms or invite questions from the floor as at a public meeting?

Garth Lean: That would be dangerous. We have such an explosive mixture of nations here.

The talk then turned on the accusation of snobbery so often levelled against Dr. Buchman.

Garth Lean: Frank is only interested in getting the best out of people. If an important man comes here Frank tries to make him realise his full responsibilities. His manner is the same with everybody. Last Sunday we had the ex-King and Queen of Rumania here. What power have they? What use could they be to us? And precisely because they have no power we treated them exactly as if they were reigning monarchs.

A. L.: I've seen Dr. Buchman receive various people at Caux from Princesses downwards, and I cannot say that I noticed any difference in his manner.

Lady Hardinge: Religion must go into every home, not only the humblest. An Anglican parson will enter a humble home where there has been a family row and try to patch things up, but he won't go into a rich home for fear of being snubbed, and yet the rich may be spiritually poor and more in need of help than the financially poor.

A. L.: The other day I was discussing Dr. Buchman with a Catholic priest. I said I believe Dr. Buchman to be a man of prayer who has dedicated himself and his life to the service of God, but I have never felt in his presence as I have felt in the presence of the very few Catholics whom I believed to be near saints. There was a numinous quality about them which was unmistakable. Colonel Hore-Ruthven, on the other hand, tells me that if you know him well you are conscious of this numinous quality. Also he said that many Asiatics revered him as a holy man.

Lady Hardinge: Many people have asked for him when they were dying, and have been very comforted to have him around.

A. L.: Let me tell you what the priest said, 'Two things are missing in his life which are present in the lives of most saints —humility and poverty.' I agreed, of course, about poverty, and it seems to me very silly to attempt to write about him as if he had no home and took all his possessions round with him in his bags. He moves from one extremely comfortable suite to the next, and when he's in Berkeley Square, Caux, Dellwood outside New York, Washington or Los Angeles, he has a delightful suite. Give him full credit for giving up a well-paid job and living on Faith till M.R.A. got moving, but today all his wants are met. If he is guided to go to Japan, somebody else is guided to buy the ticket. I've always wanted to visit Japan and I never shall. No, it's nonsense to talk about poverty in connection with Dr. Buchman. True, he does not draw a salary, but you can't eat bank notes. As to humility, I'm not so sure that the priest was right. I think he has an innocent vanity when he thinks of the world movement he has created, but I believe him to be sincere when he says that he is a striking example of what God can do, working through a quite ordinary man.

Garth Lean: He is really humble because he is convinced that anybody could do what he has done if he would yield to God and allow himself to be guided by God.

Lord Hardinge: I'm sure he's humble, and this tremendous adulation of him may not affect him, but it is bad for the general reputation of M.R.A.

A. L.: I agree. Imagine the reaction of a not too sympathetic visitor on entering the corridor above the dining-room and finding thirty-eight full-length portraits, of which eight are of Frank Buchman either alone or with other people, one repeated twice for good measure.

Garth Lean: Well, that at least we can change.[1]

On the day after this dinner I breakfasted with Lord Hardinge. He asked anxiously whether I thought he had been too out-spoken in his criticisms. I reassured him. 'It's no use criticising them,' said Hardinge, 'they do not pay the least attention.'

I had a long talk with Lady Hardinge next evening, she said, 'Every possible prejudice which you could have I have had, but what finally convinced me was the quality of life produced, their passionate conviction that any ambition or any interest which edges God out of first place is idolatrous. What really overcame my prejudices was the really saintly

[1] This has been changed—in 1956 there were only two portraits.

lives lived by so many of the MRAs. One of the things which drew me to M.R.A. was that people in it *cared* so tremendously for other people and entered so completely into their worries.'

A Swiss priest made the same point to me. What impressed him most at Caux was *Die grosse Liebe*—the great love. The first-century test, 'See how these Christians love one another', is a test which M.R.A. passes triumphantly.

Just before he left Lord Hardinge said to me that he was glad to be leaving before the World Mission returned, because he would not enjoy hearing England run down on the platform. 'These people are always asking me for advice as to how to influence the ruling classes in England, but naturally they don't take my advice. What makes M.R.A. so unpopular is that people are really shocked by the constant attribution of low motives to British administrators abroad.'

Garth Lean, with whom I discussed this conversation, said, 'I quite agree with you that we should present a balanced picture, but Hardinge does not realise how much we are disliked in these countries. He believes that it is only a few intellectuals who hate us. The hatred is there and at least our M.R.A. methods are doing something to change it.'

I raised with Basil Yates, Lord Hardinge's suggestion that criticisms should be invited from the platform.

'What is our job here?' he replied. 'The *cure* of sick souls. Would doctors stop in the middle of an operation to invite patients to criticise their methods? No, but they would of course discuss *among themselves* their mistakes and how to improve their methods.'

This seems to me reasonable. They get people at Caux for perhaps no more than a week. They have to create an atmosphere in which the newcomers are forced to admit their need to change. Psycho-analysts describe the process of inventing reasons to believe in what people want to believe as 'rationalisation'. Rationalisation is invoked to justify moral lapses, and if M.R.A. invited criticisms from the platform, those criticisms would be easily seized on by the unchanged as an excuse for not changing.

I admit that it would be a mistake to invite criticisms during the Assemblies, but what bothered me at Caux was the extreme reluctance of any M.R.A. to admit that Dr. Buchman could ever have made a mistake, even, to take one example, in the adoption of the name Oxford Group, which was an error in taste and in strategy. The contrast between Catholics and M.R.A. in this respect is shattering. 'Catholics,' as Father Martindale somewhere remarked, 'use up all their available unity on points of defined doctrine and have nothing left over for anything else.' To the outside world Catholics present a more or less united front, but among themselves there is no pretence that any aspect of, or individual in, the Catholic Church is beyond criticism.

Whereas at Caux, 'Frank's guidance is always right', would seem to be an article of faith, it is a matter of history that the Vatican has more often failed than succeeded when an attempt has been made to impose a policy which conflicted with national or class interests. The duel was condemned, but men of honour continued to fight duels. In the last war it was common knowledge among Catholics that the Vatican hoped for American intervention, but this knowledge had little or no influence on Catholics in neutral countries whose views were determined by very different considerations.[1]

Again, whereas the weak points of Catholics, both lay and clerical, are often mercilessly exposed in Catholic novels—the hero for instance of Graham Greene's *The Power and the Glory* is a drunken Mexican priest, with an illegitimate child, who none the less dies a martyr—the 'changed' characters in M.R.A. plays are always impeccable. Catholic novelists often poke fun at Catholics, clerical and lay, as for instance in Bruce Marshall's *The Miracle*, but M.R.A. have not yet learned to laugh at themselves.

MRAs lack self-confidence. They are much too nervous about what the world calls criticism, and what they call 'negatives'. Catholics in the past have suffered from the same fear of criticism, but that phase is passing. Professor J. B. S. Haldane is,

[1] To take one example. An unnamed American priest, now known to have been Monsignor Hurley, denounced on the Vatican Radio American isolationists three weeks after Italy had entered the war. The Pope appointed him Bishop of Fort St. Augustine in Florida about a month before Pearl Harbour. He had no sooner arrived than he initiated a radio campaign against isolation. For other evidence see my book *Memory to Memory*.

and the late Dr. G. G. Coulton was, a bitter enemy of the
Church, but the book consisting of an exchange of letters between Haldane and me was published in the U.S.A. by a
Catholic publisher, Sheed and Ward, and selected by the
Catholic Book of the Month Club. I found it in many Catholic
college libraries. When Dr. Coulton failed to find a Protestant
publisher for our book *Is the Catholic Church Anti-social?*, I approached Cardinal Griffin and asked him whether he would
have any objection to Burns, Oates and Washbourne, publishers to the Holy See, publishing my correspondence with
Coulton. The Cardinal, so far from objecting, thought this a
very good idea, and the book, which contained a fine confused
collection of insults, directed against the Church in general
and various Popes in particular, was on sale in the Burns and
Oates shop along with rosaries, devotional books and statues
of Our Lady.

It is, on the other hand, inconceivable that the present book,
written by a detached but friendly critic of M.R.A., would
be on sale in M.R.A. bookshops. It contains too many negatives. I did find at Caux an occasional MRA, notably Garth
Lean, Alan Thornhill, Francis Goulding and Paul Campbell,
who was ready to concede that an occasional criticism was
just. Paul Campbell, who threw up the prospects of a brilliant
medical career to join Dr. Buchman, summed up his own attitude to criticism as follows, 'If we feel that the critic understands what we are after and criticises us to make us more
effective, we accept it, but sometimes people in M.R.A. are
worried by outside criticisms and we know that the change in
our methods which they urge is really intended to make *them*
feel more comfortable and to protect *them* from outside criticism. But the other day a Lille priest told us that we should
work more through the Hierarchy in France. We immediately
saw the point of that and will do so.'

Perhaps what really gives MRAs the reputation of being
cocksure and impervious to criticism is their faith in guidance,
which in its more extreme forms is perilously near a belief in
a new kind of infallibility. Mrs. Hore-Ruthven, for instance,
said to me, 'I have often been certain that some proposal was
right, only to be met by the chilling question, "Did you get

that in guidance?" ' MRAs, therefore, are in the main unimpressed by the criticisms of the unchanged and the unguided.

It is, however, only fair to add that Peter Howard once said to me, 'I'm quite certain that God laid His hands on you and that your book is the result of His guidance, so I don't want to criticise the basic plan of the book.'

XIII

CATHOLICS AT CAUX

DURING the summers which I spent at Caux I made a point of trying to elicit the views of the priests who were ministering to the Catholics who were at Caux, or who were visiting Caux at the invitation of M.R.A. I met one priest, and only one, who was definitely unfavourable. I met two who seemed to me rather uncritical in their enthusiasm, but the great majority were in agreement on certain main points which may be summarised as follows:

(1) Whatever may be one's verdict on the different conceptions of guidance to be found among MRAs, one must respect the determination to discover God's will and to conform to that will.

(2) Those who so consistently and so sincerely seek God's guidance will be guided towards rather than away from the Church.

(3) It is therefore not surprising that non-Christians at Caux are sometimes converted to Christianity and Protestants to Catholicism.

(4) As there are many cases of lapsed Catholics returning to the Church through their contact with M.R.A., and of Protestants becoming Catholics, and no case of a Catholic becoming a Protestant, there is nothing to fear and much to hope from M.R.A.

(5) M.R.A. is creating a bridge between Catholics and Protestants, and between Christians and non-Christians.

(6) There is a definite place for a group such as M.R.A. which can build a bridge between the Christian and the non-Christian worlds. Non-Christians who are unapproachable by missionaries, and conditioned to repel any explicitly Christian advance, are co-operating in M.R.A. with Christians and are thereby slowly losing their prejudices against Christianity.

(7) As M.R.A. is a movement which includes many non-Christians it is clear that controversial issues which divide the Christians and the non-Christians in the movement have to be avoided. Furthermore, as we have seen, there is a danger that Catholics may be forbidden to be associated with M.R.A. if the movement does not confine itself strictly to co-operation on the basis of theism for social ends. It is Rome which has asked that explicitly Christian doctrines should not be discussed on M.R.A. platforms or in M.R.A. literature.

The overwhelming majority of Catholics who have spent long enough at Caux to understand the movement, accept the seven main points summarised above. But if once we admit the usefulness of a group to bridge the gap between Christians and non-Christians under the indirect influence of Christianity, we must not complain of the inevitable consequences of such a policy. Life is a choice of sacrifices, and if it be permissible for a specialist group, such as M.R.A., to co-operate with non-Christians in the attempt to create a better world, it is unjust to complain because the criterion of success adopted by M.R.A. so often seems to be purely secular objectives, such as improved relations between employers and employees, or between different races and different countries.

Historic Christianity has always seen this world against a background of tremendous urgencies, as the place of trial where a man's eternal status is decided. God became man to save sinners from Hell. This doctrine is so embedded in Christ's teaching that those who reject the possibility that a soul may be eternally lost should have the intellectual honesty to describe themselves as Unitarians.

For reasons already stated there can be no explicit reference in M.R.A. pronouncements to the salvation of souls, which is the primary motive of authentic Christianity. To the Catholic, however, M.R.A. is important not because MRAs have settled some strikes and improved relations between Europe and Africa, but because their influence has been decisive in the lives of many who ignored God before they met M.R.A., and who now daily seek His guidance. M.R.A. is a marginal force on the wing of the main army, which has its own definite if modest

role to play in the battle between Christ and anti-Christ, and
because M.R.A. must be judged to be a success by this supremely important criterion, we must not allow our judgement to be clouded by the irritation provoked by inflated
claims. It is, of course, exasperating to be assured that M.R.A.
is the only ideology which can save the world, or that the only
alternatives are M.R.A. or Communism. Dr. Buchman is not
the first prophet who has insisted that unless the world adopts
his specific remedy world ruin is inevitable. He has other rivals
in the modern world who offer us the same alternatives of
their particular panacea or destruction, Arnold Toynbee, for
instance, whose dream of world unity is offered to us as the
only alternative to world war and world ruin. *Mutatis mutandis*,
the comment of the Dutch historian Pieter Geyl on Toynbee,
is equally valid as a criticism of the less balanced prophets of
M.R.A. 'The chances of a real conversion, such as Toynbee
means, appear to me to be so exiguous that to make the survival of western civilisation depend on their being realised
would almost amount to a sentence of death.'[1]

'I'm giving most of my capital to M.R.A.,' a friend of mine
remarked, 'because I regard M.R.A. as the only alternative
to world war.' If that were so the outlook would indeed be
bleak. M.R.A. has no influence whatever behind the Iron
Curtain, where the issues of war and peace will be decided,
and no real influence on the ruling classes in any of the Western
powers.

'I'm an admirer of your Church,' a distinguished officer
remarked to me, 'but at the moment I believe that M.R.A. is
the best thing to back. For one thing we are received and
have access to circles closed to Catholics. You can't imagine
a Catholic world mission being received as ours was as honoured
guests in countries such as Pakistan or Persia or Egypt.'

'A few days ago,' I replied, 'one of your people was discussing a suggestion in the Press that Billy Graham might be invited to Moscow, and the M.R.A. comment was that M.R.A.
would never be invited because they constituted a far more
effective and explicit challenge to Communism than Billy
Graham. I agree, but isn't that also the explanation of why

[1] *Debates with Historians*, p. 138.

your World Mission is welcomed by those who might not welcome a Catholic World Mission?'

It was inevitable that the hosts of M.R.A. should vie with
each other in proclaiming how much they respected the M.R.A.
ideals. They could hardly be expected to insist that in point
of fact they themselves believed in absolute selfishness and absolute debauchery. The Governor of Ankara is quoted proudly
by Peter Howard as announcing that 'Ankara citizens as well
as the whole Turkish nation accept truthfully and eternally
your ideology.' Were the Turkish mobs who burnt and looted
the Greek shops in the Istanbul equivalent of Piccadilly and
Regent Street, inspired by absolute love? Peter Howard also
quotes Colonel Nasser's telegram in which he welcomed M.R.A.
and asserted that the principles of M.R.A. 'are highly appreciated in Egypt where all efforts are mobilised to restore moral
values, social justice, human dignity and freedom'.

The success of the M.R.A. world mission must be judged
not by the speeches of welcome addressed to the mission by
polite orientals, but by more exacting criteria, and it is still too
soon to assess the enduring influence, if any, of the World
Mission.

'You will agree, I suppose,' said my friend, 'that we have
access to circles into which Catholics could not penetrate.'

'Access perhaps, but whereas there is no race, no human
type unrepresented in the Catholic Church, many of those who
have been converted to Catholicism would find M.R.A. propaganda highly distasteful. One can't imagine Monsignor Knox
or Father Martindale or Chesterton, Christopher Dawson,
Evelyn Waugh or Graham Greene on an M.R.A. platform.
And there is one other point worth making. You send your
teams where they are welcome, and specialise in circles that
are accessible. You held no House Parties in Nazi Germany.

'In Howard's *The World Rebuilt*, there is a story of a Norwegian student who was changed at Caux. He was to have
gone as a delegate to the International Union of Students'
meeting in Prague. He decided not to go because the Western
democracies were divided and could not appear at Prague with
a common ideology. In other words, until everybody joins
M.R.A. it is no use trying to solve any of the problems of this

K

distracted planet. Did the Apostles say, "We won't go to Athens or Rome because the Jews have no common ideology. We must try to unite our own people before we spread our views elsewhere"? What a chance that boy missed to proclaim his new-found faith. Perhaps the real explanation was a failure of nerve.

'And now by way of contrast let me tell you something. More than fifty priests who were ordained in one of the Eastern Uniate rites so that they could say Mass in Russian, have gone behind the Iron Curtain. They weren't welcomed like your M.R.A. teams. On the contrary, when they were discovered they were promptly liquidated. So far as is known they are all dead.'

'What good did they do,' said my friend, 'by getting themselves killed?'

' "What good then did Priscus do, being alone?" '

'I don't follow the point.'

Priscus was the only senator to defy Vespasian, and he was executed. The quotation is from Epictetus, 'What good then did Priscus do, being alone? Only the good that the purple thread in the toga does by showing up the commonplaceness of the rest.'

In the economy of God the death of one martyr may achieve far more than the two hundred and forty-four people from twenty-eight countries who travelled round with the M.R.A. World Mission. It is only fair to add that next day my friend came to me and said, 'I'm sorry I made that silly remark yesterday about those priests who went into Russia. They were dedicated men.'

It is because their terms of reference exclude any emphasis on the basic Christian doctrine, that this world is a preparation for the next, that MRAs so often give an impression, which does not really correspond to the best thought in the movement, of being exclusively concerned with the criterion of *visible* success in this world. There is a story of a Catholic missionary which I told more than once at Caux and which is a useful corrective to the kind of success story typical of M.R.A.

This missionary worked for twenty years somewhere on the

Indian frontier without making a single convert, and on his death-bed he wrote to the Superior of his Order to warn him that it would be a waste of time to appoint a successor. A few days after his death another message was sent from the tribe asking for a successor to be appointed. They explained that they had been so impressed by the tenacity with which the missionary had continued to proclaim what he believed to be true that they had come to the conclusion that there must be something very real about a religion which could inspire a man to treat apparent failure with such contempt. They had therefore decided to ask for baptism.

Priests at Caux

I made a careful note of many of my conversations with priests at Caux, and here are some extracts from records made within a few hours of the conversations recorded.

A Jesuit, Father Trösch, who is a student chaplain at Basle University, said to me, 'Caux is a challenge to us Catholics. I ask myself why I do not get as impressive results with my students at Basle as they get at Caux, I, who have all the treasures of the Church to draw on, compared to their primitive methods. Their plays, for instance, are hardly more sophisticated than the Jesuit plays of the seventeenth century at Brigue.'

Father Seiler, who came to Caux deeply prejudiced, was most impressed by what they have achieved. 'Of course, for us Catholics with our long memories we can see all sorts of tendencies at work here which the Church has known in the past. In M.R.A. we can find traces of that excessive rigorism in their attitude not only to wine but also to sex, which we have met before in earlier heresies, Manichaeism and Catharism for instance, and what is creating a real problem for the Catholic full-timers is sharing guidance with non-Catholics. There is a Catholic girl here who misbehaved in the past, and the team tell her that she is not absolutely honest because she won't tell her mother about her lapse. We know that it is often a mistake to confess things which the other party does not know. A wife, for instance, may forgive a husband who confesses, but the wound remains. In that particular case absolutely nothing would be gained by telling the mother. Then again, a team may be guided to tell a married couple, after their first baby has arrived, to live as brother and sister, and this again creates problems. Rome does not want Protestants exercising a kind of moral jurisdiction over Catholics. On the other hand, M.R.A. do not want separate Catholic teams which introduces religious divisions which they want to avoid.'

I asked him for his forecast of the future.

'Probably within fifty years M.R.A. will have vanished, like so many movements outside the Church, but there are other possibilities. The informed Catholics in M.R.A., because they have so many centuries of spiritual experience to draw on, will gradually check and correct the raw excesses of guidance and they may in time exercise great influence. That will in turn provoke a strong Protestant reaction which may split the movement.

'But for the moment we owe it to M.R.A., which has shown such good will towards the Church, to co-operate so far as we can. This is a world movement and provides us with a platform, and we must not draw aside. I am struck by the large number of Catholics who come back to the Church as the result of their contact with M.R.A.'

Two days later I lunched with Paul Campbell. He was shocked when I quoted the priest as criticising Protestants in M.R.A. for trying to force their guidance on Catholics.

'Nobody has any business in trying to force their guidance on other people, but I can see how it happens. I was once a very ambitious doctor. I was determined to get to the top. That and sex were my problems. Sex I've conquered. I keep the margins.'

'Margins? What's that?'

'The margin between temptation and me. There are certain books and magazines I won't even glance at, but ambition to get to the top persists in all of us in subtle forms. As for instance in the determination to force our guidance on other people.'

Next day Father Trösch, the Jesuit, Paul Campbell and I lunched together. We discussed guidance.

Paul Campbell: My definition of guidance would be 'My best thoughts under the guidance of God.'

Father Trösch: What worries us is Catholics submitting to the moral jurisdiction of Protestants, as for instance when a Protestant member of a team tells a Catholic what their guidance for them is.

Paul Campbell: The more advanced a man is in M.R.A. the less will he be tempted to impose his guidance on others. For instance, we never say here, 'Give up smoking and drinking.'

Father Trösch: Perhaps not, but the pressure of the climate of opinion is irresistible. How did you come to join M.R.A.?

Paul Campbell: In my case it was just as if God had taken me by the scruff of the neck and jerked me out of the hospital in which a good appointment was waiting for me, and I've been on the road ever since.

I had tea the same day with Father Trösch. 'What worries me,' he said, 'is not Dr. Campbell's conception of guidance, which is reasonable. There is a close relationship between their conception and the Ignatian. But the line which separates the reasonable and the unreasonable conception is subtle and easily crossed. With these advanced MRAs like Mottu and Campbell one feels reassured, but there appears to be no control on the less advanced and it is this that worries the Church.'

At that moment a charming middle-aged lady came up and gave us tea. I asked her whether she was an American. 'No, I'm from Toronto, but we feel very close to the Americans because of Frank Buchman. America needs change, but we need it more.'

Father Trösch sighed as she left. 'That is typical of the kind of fanaticism which irks one here. M.R.A. has to be dragged into any conversation however trivial. And the constant *Druck* (pressure—we were talking German) is out of proportion.

'There is a nice Dutch couple here, both Catholics. The woman is a very good Catholic and has devoted her life to Catholic activities and good works. "I know I'm not a saint," she said to me, "or anything remotely like a saint, but I've tried to live a decent Catholic life, and when I come here everybody tells me I've got to change, and that some radical revolution is necessary. They just won't leave my husband and me in peace." Or take myself. Like Dr. Campbell, I did not want to follow my vocation. I went into the Order reluctantly, but God called me and there was no turning back. Every year I do the Spiritual Exercises for a week. All the time I am fighting to avoid religion becoming a routine and to advance spiritually. The advance is of course slow and difficult, but with the very best will in the world I cannot see what revolutionary change they are expecting from me.'

(I mentioned this conversation to Campbell, who agreed at once that Father Trösch was not in need of change as change is understood at Caux.)

We went on to talk about the contrast between the optimism of M.R.A. which I have defined as moral utopianism, and the realism of the Church.

Father Trösch: We know only too well that the Devil is permitted again and again to bring to nothing the best efforts of good and holy people. In Paraguay the Jesuits had built up a splendid social order which is admired to this day by historians, and then it all came to nothing. And so it will be to the end of time. There is no hope of perfection on earth. None the less, we Catholics have to do our utmost as if indeed we believed that utopia was just round the corner, and accept defeat as the will of God. St. Ignatius was once asked how long it would take him to recover if the Order were dissolved, and he came to the conclusion that it would take him fifteen minutes to readjust himself. And when the Order was dissolved in the eighteenth century the Jesuits behaved admirably and did their best to serve God as secular priests. But, I ask myself, would M.R.A. behave as well if the material structure collapsed as the result of some financial crisis?

A. L.: Yes, I have often wondered what would be the reaction of those who have been deflected by M.R.A. from learning a profession.

Father Trösch: This naïve optimism, this conviction that M.R.A. has the key which can solve all the problems of the world is dangerous. It is perhaps even tinged with a certain kind of materialism, as if material results in this world were the ultimate test of success, the settling of strikes, etc., and here again we have another source of discomfort. I give

CATHOLICS AT CAUX 151

M.R.A. full credit for bringing back so many lapsed or indifferent Catholics to the practice of their Faith, but the more deeply they begin to understand their own Faith the more worried they are by this naïve optimism of M.R.A. One of our Catholics here, when he speaks on M.R.A. platforms, tries to introduce a note of reality, but it is not well received. One sometimes feels at these Assemblies as if there were an unavowed intention to stifle the reason and escape from the real world and its problems.

It may be that this naïve optimism is an essential condition for the survival of the movement. In 1933 Alan Thornhill, a former Fellow and Chaplain of Hertford College, Oxford, could write in his attractive biography of Canon B. F. Streeter, 'England in her own characteristic way was slowly and often reluctantly taking the Group to her heart.' A hopeful estimate which the years have done nothing to confirm. But the Group goes on and seems as confident today as in 1933 that the future is theirs. It remains to be seen whether the movement will survive the discovery that the world as a whole will never accept the guidance of Dr. Buchman, and whether the MRAs will resign themselves to the modest role of a small but effective unit in an army waging a never-ending war against the legions of anti-Christ.

That same night I dined with Richard Stollery, a Canadian, and another Canadian who confirmed what I have already mentioned, the fact that the Trieste team, there being no Protestant service, went to Mass every Sunday and were held up as examples by the priest. On the subject of guidance, Stollery said, 'Sometimes when I've tried to change somebody it has been my success in changing him that has been the dominant motive, and this is not a valid motive. The only valid motive is to respond to a man's deepest needs.' Stollery was interested that Catholics were concerned that Protestants should go to church. I said: 'There are two issues. One, if only a small proportion of your full-timers attend church on Sunday the inference is that you feel you do not need the ministrations of a Church because you are, consciously or unconsciously, developing into a Quaker-like sect of your own.

Two, we believe that the corporate act of worship on Sundays is a duty of respect which man owes to his Creator, and that M.R.A. should help to arrest the decline of public worship.'

It was clear to me from other discussions that one reason for the poor church attendance is that many of these MRAs are very close to the Catholic Church, and are therefore dissatisfied with Protestant services. The thing which holds many back from the final stage of submitting to Rome is the fear that Rome may condemn M.R.A.

The Jesuits are theoretically forbidden in Switzerland, but an occasional Jesuit is tolerated, Father Seiler, for instance, who like Father Trösch, is a university chaplain, and a grandson of Alexander Seiler of Zermatt. We saw a lot of each other. He often repeated that M.R.A. was *Eine grosse Phenomene* (A great phenomenon), and it was Father Seiler who, when I asked him what struck him most at Caux, replied, *Die grosse Liebe*, the great love which MRAs had for their fellow men. He began by trying to dissuade me from writing this book and then one day, quite spontaneously, said, 'I have come to the conclusion that your book on M.R.A. will be valuable in clearing away confusions.'

He had changed his view about Dr. Buchman. At first he thought he was too old to face unwelcome facts, but the speed with which he reacted to the danger of a condemnation from Rome of M.R.A., and the admirable statement he issued later to the effect that M.R.A. was only a gateway to a church, and that MRAs should check their guidance with their own spiritual directors, proved that his mind was as alert as ever.

'He has,' said Father Seiler, 'a marvellous memory and an immense insight and feeling for the individual.'

We agreed that he summed up people pretty quickly and did not waste any time on the unchangeable. Mr. Williamson's book *Inside Buchmanism* contains a brilliant bit of reporting in which he describes Dr. Buchman's bored and impassive reaction when Mr. Williamson said goodbye. Dr. Buchman was in bed when he called.

> One nude foot protruded stiffly from beneath the disarranged bedclothes. . . . Why, I wondered, had Dr. Buchman elected to exhibit himself to me without his cloak? . . .

As I approached the bedside, avoiding the sentinel of that out-stretched foot, Dr. Buchman extended a hand, semi-deformed with arthritis. But he remained silent. His acolytes were silent. I was silent. The situation was so grotesquely different from anything I had conjured up in my mind's eye that I was non-plussed. I have been ushered into the presence of many famous personalities in my time, but I had never experienced a reception quite like this.

At last, to break the prolonged tension, I blurted some words of thanks for all the hospitality I had received. . . .

'Fine!' murmured Dr. Buchman with no show of interest. Again an awful silence descended upon the room. I wanted to be bold without appearing rude.

'They're keeping the coach waiting for me,' I said. 'So I must say goodbye. But I'm taking back a lot of interesting impressions of Caux; some of them very deep impressions.' But even this flowery farewell failed to draw the slightest response beyond a repeated murmur of 'Fine!' Dr. Buchman's face was a mask of almost Oriental inscrutability.

So I retreated in confusion.

Father Trösch and Father Sieler were Catholic chaplains to the universities of Basle and Zürich respectively, and I was interested to compare their views with those of an Italian chaplain to the University of Bologna, a most able man whose name I unfortunately forgot to record. The town of Bologna is very Red, but a friend of the university chaplain had taken down more than one group of Communists to see the saintly Padre Pio, and they had all returned converted as we say, or changed as the MRAs would say.

'The Cardinal,' said this priest, 'has sent me here to make a report. He says, "We must judge M.R.A. by its fruits. If the fruits are good why condemn it?"

'So far there has not been a single apostasy from the Church, and there have even been some vocations to the priesthood. The Holy Office will therefore be very slow to condemn and will, I am sure, take no such step for some years, and mean-while we must find a *modus vivendi*. The Holy Office have now forbidden Catholics to accept a leading role in M.R.A. They don't want them to go on the World Mission and were edi-fied when two Catholics immediately withdrew. We are not happy about Catholics sharing guidance with non-Catholics, among other reasons because this movement is deeply infected by puritanism.'

The Italian priest continued:

'Some of my Italian young men come here and complain that they feel under surveillance. There was always one of the full-time workers around. They felt they were being watched like a patient whose temperature is taken every hour. "Have you changed? Why don't you change? Lose no time. Change."'

But in spite of all this his verdict was favourable.

Another priest said to me: 'Nothing is more striking than the contrast between the readiness with which MRAs admit their own individual mistakes, and their reluctance to admit that Dr. Buchman or M.R.A. has ever made any mistakes, and this is not at all sensible because every Catholic who comes into contact with M.R.A. knows very well that mistakes in leadership have been made, just as we know that our leaders have sometimes been mistaken.'

Catholics who are content to judge Caux from a distance and whose approach to the problem is deductive rather than inductive, often write as if cordiality between Catholics and other Christians must lead to indifferentism. I have discussed this question with many priests who visited Caux and who have taken the trouble to study the movement. They are firm and united on these two points. First, that no Catholic has ever received guidance at Caux to leave the Church, and secondly, that the Catholics who seek guidance are invariably guided to become better Catholics.

I made friends at Caux with a remarkable priest, Abbé Verscheure, of Lille. I was impressed by the clarity of his mind and the exactness with which he clarified the issues.

> I tell Catholics who are critical [he said] to come to Caux and when they come to Caux I suggest that they should try to live the life of M.R.A. I know many Catholics who are full-time workers and there is not one whose spiritual life has not been deepened by contact with M.R.A.

And then he continued in words which he allows me to quote:

Je n'ai jamais rencontré un prêtre qui ait connu un seul catholique devenu moins convaincu à la suite de sa pratique le Re-Armement Moral est un fait, et non une théorie. Evidement il y a une certaine théorie qui informe ce fait; mais il est inexact d'imaginer que l'on peut analyser le fait en étudiant la théorie; et il faut voir le fait autrement que dans les écrits ou certaines affirmations; il faut voir la vie sans le R.A.M. On constate d'ailleurs sur place que le role d'observateur est difficile a remplir sans soi-même vivre la phenomène R.A.M. On rencontrera de multiples formulations orales et même écrites, qui sont inexactes du point de vue de la théologie Catholique; mais si l'on veut bien dépasser les mots, rechercher la pensée, interroger afin de trouver la pensée, on constatera presque toujours que la pensée n'est jamais contraire explicitement à la théologie Catholique, bien qu'elle soit souvent incomplete.[1]

[1] Translation provided and authorised by Abbé Verscheure: 'I have never met a single priest who has ever known a single Catholic who has become less convinced as the result of the practice of M.R.A. M.R.A. is a fact and not a theory. Evidently there is a certain theory which informs this fact, but it is incorrect to imagine that one can analyse this Fact in studying the theory. One must examine this fact otherwise than in the writings or in certain statements of M.R.A. One must observe it in the life of M.R.A. One discovers that the role of an observer is difficult without oneself living the life of M.R.A. One meets many verbal statements and written ones which are inexact from the point of view of Catholic theology, but if one penetrates beyond the words to the thoughts and even cross-examines them to discover the thought, one almost always discovers that the thought is not explicitly contrary to Catholic theology even if it be often incomplete.'

XIV

ROME AND M.R.A.

As the English Hierarchy have made it clear that they
disapprove of a Catholic *participating* in M.R.A., I
must begin by defining my own position. It is essential that Catholics should be well informed about important
religious movements, and it was for this reason that Douglas
Woodruff, the Editor of *The Tablet*, paid a visit to Caux, and
that I am writing this book. Many of the most useful books
about non-Catholic religions have been written by Catholics,
and I recall with gratitude my debt to a Catholic priest,
Father Maximin Piette, whose admirable study of John
Wesley I read with great profit while I was at work on my
own biography of the founder of Methodism. Clearly I am
entitled to choose M.R.A. as the subject for a book, and not
only entitled but under an obligation to undertake the necessary research to ensure that the book is as good as possible.
Nothing of real value can be written on the basis of a week in
Caux. In my own case there was a further obligation. My previous essay on M.R.A. was, as I now recognise, unjust and
according to the accepted principles of Catholic theology I owe
M.R.A. such reparation as is in my power to make.

I have never felt tempted to disregard our Bishops' objection to Catholics *participating* in M.R.A. and have not parti-
cipated. Meanwhile my own view is that English Catholics
who are resident in England are bound by the ruling against
participation. If the Church militant be not a mere figure of
speech there must be authority and there must be discipline.
I remember a discussion on this point during a dinner at
Mürren. Field Marshal Viscount Montgomery turned to my
wife, his first cousin, and said, 'You and I can go to Arnold's
Mass but he can't come to our Mattins.' On which I made

the obvious comment, 'The Catholic Church is like the Eighth Army. It has discipline and a leader.'

One thing puzzles me about Catholic critics of M.R.A. I had always understood that it was a grave matter for a Catholic to reject the verdict of a Bishop about the religious movements in his own diocese, and that one was only free to differ from such a verdict after giving it the most anxious and respectful consideration. But Catholics who dislike M.R.A. sweep aside as irrelevant the views of the Bishop of Lausanne,

> Cette méthod traduit en acte un des principes essentials de la morale chrétienne. Elle a produit des résultats excellents. On a vu à Caux se réconcilier pour un labeur désormais constructif des patrons et des ouvriers jusque-là séparés par la méfiance et la haine. On a vu des catholiques et des protestants rechercher sincèrement le moyen de faire converger leurs efforts pour reconstuire l'unité chrétienne. Comment ne pas se réjouir de tout cela?[1]

I am not surprised to learn that M.R.A. is being attacked in certain American Protestant circles as destructive of the barriers which separate Protestants from Catholicism. But that Catholics should attack a movement which is responsible for the return of so many lapsed Catholics is indeed depressing.

Broadly speaking I believe it to be true that most of the many Bishops who have allowed their priests to visit Caux are far from hostile to M.R.A. The Cardinal Bishop of Lille, for instance, was deeply impressed by the beneficent influence of M.R.A. on some of the industrialists in his own diocese, with the result that he sent many of his own priests to Caux.

I should, as a layman, hesitate to express my own views on M.R.A. if these differed radically from the Catholic priests who have first-hand experience of the movement, but this is not the case. Of all the Catholic priests at Caux with whom I have discussed M.R.A., *not one* desired the condemnation of M.R.A. by Rome, and only one was severe in his judgements.

I am reassured to discover how closely my own views on

---

[1] This method gives practical expression to one of the fundamental principles of Christian morality. It has achieved excellent results. Caux has brought together in constructive effort employers and workers who have hitherto felt only mistrust and hatred for one another. Catholics and Protestants are there seen sincerely seeking the means of joint action to rebuild Christian unity. How can anyone fail to welcome this with joy?

M.R.A. coincide with those of twelve priests, from five different countries, who met at Lausanne towards the end of March, 1954, under the chairmanship of Monsignor Charrière, Bishop of Lausanne, Geneva and Fribourg, in whose diocese Caux is situated. Their report has never been published and has, of course, no official character, but I am grateful for permission to quote from it.

Twelve Priests Report on M.R.A.

The twelve priests who met in Lausanne under the chairmanship of the Bishop of Lausanne begin with a very necessary reminder that 'M.R.A. cannot be discovered through its literature. It must be approached "existentially".' After a brief summary of the history of M.R.A. and its basic principles, they continue:[1]

Moral Re-Armament is completely *unprejudiced towards the various confessions* and religious opinions. It has often been noted that in Moral Re-Armament '*Protestants do not protest any more.*' Frank Buchman himself, when still working as a minister, helped lukewarm Catholics to rekindle their faith, to go back to their priests and to take up their sacramental practices again. Other clergy have copied him since. There is similarly complete understanding towards the followers of other religions, Hindus, Muslims, etc., and even atheists. From the moment that a person of goodwill chooses to practise Moral Re-Armament, he can share in its activities without being asked to explain his religious convictions, or how he reconciles them with the quiet time. It is a fact that numerous Christians have been brought, or brought back, by Moral Re-Armament, to a practising and even fervent Catholicism, some coming from non-Catholic Christian confessions, and an apparently even larger number issuing from a state of indifference or of religious mediocrity. Atheists have found faith. Is there any movement in the other direction? No definite instance exists which would allow us to think so.

It might seem prima facie that Moral Re-Armament's welcoming attitude towards all religious opinions might create a religious indifferentism amongst its members. The facts do not seem to confirm this fear. They point to the exact contrary, at least as far as Catholics are concerned. It does seem as if some

[1] The italics in my quotations are mine.

non-Catholic Christians do leave their denomination or at least drop its practice. Do they think that they will find God better or serve Him better in Moral Re-Armament?

This would, however, be overstating the case. We must recall that regular attendance at church has not for Protestants the importance it has for us, and that the Sacraments occupy only a minor place in their lives. *In point of fact Moral Re-Armament does not foster indifferentism among Catholics and their sacramental life does not lose its fervour.* Of course, we are speaking here of people who have lived the life of Moral Re-Armament over a long period and not of vague sympathisers or new beginners who may have a very poor and still imperfect understanding of it.

The Report then discusses Caux:

. . . Some are charmed and some are irritated by its atmosphere. Some people have had the impression that their liberty is being curtailed by means of kindliness, gentleness, propaganda, and that they are not left adequate time or a favourable setting for thought. To understand Moral Re-Armament properly, and, *a fortiori*, to judge it fairly, it is essential to rise above these unthinking reactions. Since it sets out to be a mass movement, it employs means adapted to set people on the move. These means might cause disquiet if their aims were covert or dishonest, if they were misleading about the real nature of Moral Re-Armament, but not if all they did was to make it accessible to everybody, even at the risk of arousing the susceptibilities of the sensitive. To such sensitive people Caux offers personal contacts with the leaders, whose moral level and quality of spirit create the atmosphere and are even more appreciated in such personal encounters.

As to Finance, the Report continues:

There is nothing mysterious, especially for us Catholics, in the finances, which are run just like our works of charity, entirely by gifts and free-will offerings. The leaders constantly make it clear that they have nothing to hide. What is less known is that the full-time workers live a very exacting and effective personal poverty, however unexpected its form might be for us.

The Report emphasises the importance of Catholics being associated with M.R.A.:

. . . Quite apart from our faith in the promises of eternal life, we feel that the Catholic Church is the only universal organisation in the realm of moral forces and that if she closes her gates to Moral Re-Armament, Moral Re-Armament would be checked in its desire for world-wide action. Vice versa, it is easy to see what interest the outcome of this development would have for the Church. Here is a moral force working on a world scale. *If its activity can ally itself with that of the Church, if there are no doctrinal incompatibilities, it is of foremost importance that Catholics should take part in it.* No one, whatever his approach, is unaware of the significance and scope of this question.

What is new [the Report asks] in Moral Re-Armament? . . .

Something totally new seems to be here present, something totally original compared with all previous movements which some have wanted to cite as analogies to Moral Re-Armament. Attempts have been made to regard Moral Re-Armament as a revival of the type of which there have been many instances in Protestantism, but no single one of these movements in the past has ever overflowed the bounds of Protestantism. Attempts have been made to paint Moral Re-Armament as an emanation of Freemasonry. But Freemasonry had a religious doctrine, well-developed and differing from country to country. It has sought to impose its doctrine, sometimes even claiming to become a sort of super-church; and above all each of the different Masonic Lodges has pursued political aims and worked to establish the hegemony of a dynasty or a group. With Moral Re-Armament appears a force without the slightest claim to the doctrinal and religious leadership of the world, without the slightest sign of imperialism or political ambition. (It is so long since the accusation of covert aims was launched that had it had any positive foundation the evidence would have been produced by now.) Its only aim is to move to the aid of a sick world on the moral level.

Have the leaders of Moral Re-Armament intentionally chosen a new way? This question may not be the most important one. What is of capital importance is that *up till now they have been able to live out a genuine universalism because they have been ready for any personal sacrifice that the next step of obedience to this end demanded* and in particular that they have been able to free themselves from becoming a confessional movement. This fact must be recognised; and there is nothing in its historical antecedents which would lead us to imagine that this line of development had been decided on beforehand or inscribed in the nature of things. It seems on the contrary that at every stage the leaders have been faced with a choice between divergent roads and often have had to guard against falling back into the ruts of the past. The internal necessity which drove them was a living purpose. It has been a kind of vocation; every sort of temptation, even the times when they might have let their purpose degenerate to ambition, has only served to recall them to their sense of mission with an ever sharper awareness.

The Report then discusses what M.R.A. is not:

... *It is not a religion, a church or a sect.* It has neither dogma, hierarchy nor liturgy. It refrains from all strict religious teaching and exhorts the Christian to seek his religious training and development in his Church. Nor can it be said to claim to be a super-church. The respect with which it treats the religious hierarchies, and the Catholic Church in particular, precludes such a claim. Thus, it does not operate either on a super-confessional or inter-confessional level. It does not seek to achieve unity between the Christian confessions nor to get them together on a minimum creed. The plane on which it acts is quite simply non-confessional. It does not organise meetings of a strictly religious character. It does not practise the offering of prayers aloud corporately. Prayer is always a time of silence which allows everyone to pray in his own way. ...

The Report continues that M.R.A. is an ideology:

... The word seems somewhat vague at first sight, yet the leaders of Moral Re-Armament insist upon it. *It emphasises the immense importance which they attach to the 'war of ideas', holding that ideas run the world.* ...

The Report sees in M.R.A. a natural ally of the Church:

... Operating thus on the level of natural morality, Moral Re-Armament cannot, normally, come into conflict with the Catholic Church. On the one hand it does not substitute itself for Her, and on the other *its action on men allies itself with that of the Church.* The last Popes, notably in the Social Encyclicals and the Christmas messages, have quite often *appealed to all men of good-will, even non-Christians,* for an action with moral and social aims that strictly speaking does not stem from the Christian ideal but from a natural human ideal. Finally by an inner logic, a logic of life and not of thought, it is quite obvious that many

L

people, after being morally straightened out by Moral Re-Armament and put in contact with God, the Source of moral life, should be led on to find faith in Christ, membership in the Church and all that is involved. Human nature, as such, far from being closed to the supernatural, is open to God; and moral recovery dispels great obstacles to faith. . . .

The Report then deals with the criticism that—

. . . Moral Re-Armament makes no distinction between the grave and the venial (importance attached to smoking), that some of its representatives lack wisdom in giving categorical advice that might be open to question on matters such as loyalty (confession of past failures to wife or even to children) or of purity (conjugal continence).

It would be wrong to crystallise Moral Re-Armament's attitude by forgetting that its concern is to act and to exhort more than to define or to weigh responsibilities, *or by attributing an act of some full-time worker to the movement in general*. Still it must be recognised that a problem does arise at this point. The very word absolute can contribute to confusion. For us Catholics it raises the thought of God Himself, the only absolute, the perfection unattainable by man. In Moral Re-Armament it appears to have a more practical than a metaphysical value. It expresses the firm determination to banish all compromise and even all complexity in the moral life, too complicated solutions being easily suspect. . . .

The Report discusses the different approach of the Catholic to guidance, quiet time, etc., and concludes:

. . . The fact is that we find that many Catholics owe much to the practice of the quiet time, thanks to which they have re-animated their Christian life in a spirit in full conformity with the Church's teaching. It would be highly regrettable to reject this contribution. . . .

On one point the Report is more indulgent to what I have called 'moral Utopianism' than the present writer or some of the priests which whom he has discussed this point:

. . . Individual change must lead to *world transformation*. On this point Moral Re-Armament is charged with giving in to the temptation of an *earthly Messianism*. . . .

... No human hope has more value than that which is founded on love and reconciliation between people. It would not be very Christian to invoke Original Sin in order to discourage people who want to work for the terrestrial happiness of their brethren. Christian Hope does not require us to despair of this present life. Moral Re-Armament's optimism may seem a bit naïve. To understand it, it must be looked at, not from a speculative viewpoint but from the practical angle as a force for efficiency, a state of mind which considerably increases the chances of success. This too is well in line with its nature as a force for moral action. ...

The Report then makes a point which every Protestant in M.R.A. would gladly concede, that M.R.A. is insufficient for Catholics, but adds:

... No doubt a general conclusion would be premature, but it seems legitimate to think that, Moral Re-Armament not being a religion or a religious sect, the question of 'communicatio in sacris' does not arise. On the other hand it has no dogmatic teaching, and no heresy or recognisable error has been discovered in it. ...

... Experience makes it possible to say that the results of the contacts of Catholics with Moral Re-Armament are happy. ...

... But we should be committing a grave error if we only look at it from our own viewpoint, or only consider the advantages or dangers which Moral Re-Armament might contain for ourselves. The mere presence of Catholics has already made itself widely felt and exercised a very happy influence on the development of the movement. It would be a further error for the priests who go to Caux with the approbation of the Catholic hierarchy to think that they go there solely for the Catholics. Non-Catholic full-time workers are very open to their influence and to their advice. Many of them admire the doctrinal thoroughness of Catholicism and the resources of the sacramental life. ...

The Report concludes with some very valuable recommendations to Catholics in M.R.A., and with a tribute to Dr. Buchman:

... It is of interest to note that Dr. Buchman's work has for more than forty years been effective in bringing about the return of Catholics to their Faith.

'Accurate Knowledge and Charitable Interpretation'

It was at the suggestion of Douglas Woodruff, Editor of *The Tablet*, that in 1954 I wrote an article on Caux which provoked a lively correspondence. Among those who contributed interesting letters may be mentioned Father Francis McGowan, who, among other things, said:

> It might help some of your readers who want to find out a little more about M.R.A. to know of a book written in January last year by the Auxiliary Bishop of Malines. It is called *Que faut-il penser du Réarmement moral?*, and is published by Les Editions Universitaires, Paris.
>
> Amongst other things, Mgr. Suenens suggests an answer to what has been to me a most intriguing problem, namely, that the Catholic clergy and laity in England are not at all impressed by M.R.A., whereas their brethren on the Continent have been very active in its favour, until various Bishops began to forbid it. He points out, something of which we are very conscious, that when a Catholic and a non-Catholic are talking about Christ, the Redemption, the Sacraments, etc., they very probably have a very different understanding of these things. . . .

To this I replied:

> . . . I cannot agree that continental Catholics are less alive to the effect of modernism, or worse theologians, than our own; and I make this statement with some confidence because, since my conversion, I have visited every country in Europe excepting Russia, and discussed these problems with priests in very many of these countries.
>
> The contrast between the Catholics who condemn and the Catholics who (with reservations) support M.R.A. is not that the former know more about Protestants, but that the latter know more about M.R.A. . . .

I have found more interest in, and tentative sympathy for, M.R.A. among English Catholics than Father McGowan's letter suggests. Archbishop Roberts, for instance, in the course of a review of Peter Howard's book, *The World Rebuilt*, wrote:

> The number of Catholics quoted as favourable to the Moral Re-Armament movement shows—and the fact is not surprising —that Catholics can and should be edified and inspired by the

successful application of Catholic principles, even by non-Catholics, to the social and international problems of the day.

To the Apostles scandalised by the effective labours of one not even (yet) a disciple, our Lord said that they ought to be glad, for everyone not against Him was for Him.

May Catholics study the astonishing results obtained by Moral Re-Armament and ask themselves whether they have really begun to use, for example, the sacrament of penance as our Lord intended.

In a subsequent letter to *The Tablet* the Archbishop wrote:

I know too little about the movement to justify any conviction; for reasons of prudence, I did not accept an informal invitation to Caux.

It is, perhaps, added justification of your correspondence on M.R.A., and of Sir Arnold Lunn's letters especially, that stress has been laid on the paramount claims of accurate knowledge and charitable interpretation in any Christian judgement.

On the other hand I agree with Father McGowan that continental Catholics have in general been far more favourable to M.R.A. than Catholics in the English-speaking world. But surely it is no cause for rejoicing that a splendid English convert to the Church is being ordained in France because he is not prepared to break with those to whom, under God, he owes his conversion to the Church. I could wish ecclesiastical authority would unbend to the small extent of indicating to those in the movement that they would not be required to give up their work and break with M.R.A. if they became Catholics. This fear, I know, is holding some of them back from the Church.

Instead of, for instance, arguing that M.R.A. *must* lead to indifferentism, that is to the theory that it is a matter of indifference to which Church one belongs, why not substitute the inductive for the deductive method and go to the evidence to discover whether in point of fact Catholics in M.R.A. are infected with this heresy. The facts, of course, are that whereas there have been many conversions to the Catholic Church in M.R.A., there is not one case, as I have already pointed out, of a Catholic becoming a Protestant under the influence of

Caux. In this connection it is relevant to quote an Oratorian priest, Father Crowdy, who wrote as follows:

Perhaps one who had many years' experience of M.R.A. before becoming a Catholic, and later a priest, may be permitted to express his appreciation of Sir Arnold Lunn's article.

Others besides myself have had the experience that M.R.A. can be a preparation for accepting the authority of the Church. It is also, I submit, a subject of interest for two other reasons. There are a good number of born Catholics for whom their contact with M.R.A. has made real for the first time some of the implications of the Faith (which accounts, as I know, for the friendly interest in it of at least one Bishop). Secondly, M.R.A. provides, in regions where there are numbers of Catholics working in it, a means by which they can co-operate with others for social and moral ends with effectiveness and entire mutual confidence; and I suggest that any solution of this vexed problem deserves attention.

For understanding M.R.A., I would urge the importance of personal contact. It does not fall easily into any of our usual categories, and it is not easy to grasp it from reading only.

By Hook and by Crook

On the evening before Monsignor Ronald Knox received me into the Catholic Church he produced in the course of our conversation a suggestive dichotomy. Priests, he said, might be divided into those who had a natural vocation for seeking out the unconverted, fishermen of souls, and those who were shepherds rather than fishermen, primarily concerned with their own flocks.

'The Church gets on by hook and by crook, by the hook of the fisherman and the crook of the shepherd,' and he added, 'as for myself, I'm more of a crook than a hook.'

Of course, if our only concern is to insure the faithful against the infection of heresy, many of the arguments used by critics of M.R.A. are valid. Even so, it is difficult to understand why any Catholic should be at pains to prove what nobody in M.R.A. would for one moment deny, that 'sharing' is not the same thing as sacramental confession. Of course it is not, but is that any reason for discouraging Protestants who do not avail themselves of the Sacrament of Penance from confessing their sins to each other? Inigo Lopez, whom the world now knows as St. Ignatius of Loyola, when he was helping to defend the fortress at Pamplona confessed his sins to one of his companions in arms. There was no priest in the fortress.

'In such circumstances,' writes Father Broderick, 'it was a mediaeval custom, regarded benevolently by St. Thomas Aquinas and other moral theologians, to confess one's sins to a lay person. It showed humility and good will, and would have helped to true contrition. Of course the act was in no sense sacramental.'

M.R.A. is a *hairesis* but it is not a heresy. The word *hairesis*, from which 'heresy' is derived, literally means 'choosing'. But the word 'heresy' has acquired the meaning not only of choosing but of rejecting those Catholic doctrines which are not chosen. M.R.A. chooses certain basic principles, which every Catholic can accept, but the most hostile of M.R.A.'s critics have failed to detect anything heretical in the principles which are proclaimed in its literature and on the platform at Caux.

Of course M.R.A. is defective from the Catholic point of view, but to one who is temperamentally a 'hook', this is not a reason for staying away from Caux, but a reason for being present. Our missionaries should be present not only *in partibus infidelium* but also *in partibus semi fidelium*.

In my experience the verdict of individual Catholics on M.R.A. is largely decided by whether they favour a 'catacomb' policy of isolating Catholics, so far as possible, from the danger of infection by heresy, or the policy of Catholics being present everywhere where they are welcomed and needed. To the latter the incompleteness of the M.R.A. approach is a reason, not for withdrawing in disdain, but for helping those who have found so many Christian truths to discover the Church.

My wife and I were both impressed by the contrast between the M.R.A. House Party which we attended in 1939 and the atmosphere at Caux last year, and I, at least, attribute part of this change for the better to the steady influence of the Catholics in the movement. There is, for instance, far less of that uncritical faith in detailed guidance than there was in 1939.

A French lady who had the melancholy task of looking after

my room said to me, 'I came back to the Faith at Caux. Caux has a great need of Catholics, but we must help them with humility. We have the riches of the Faith but rich people who give without humility to the poor often do more harm than good.' Indeed, Caux has a great need of Catholics. Once again I met at Caux an Anglican who assured me that he was drawn towards the Church but nervous of committing himself so long as M.R.A. was regarded with distrust by the ecclesiastical authorities. A young man who is feeling the pull of the Church went for a long walk with me during which I hope I was able to help him. Again and again one has the chance of clearing up some misconception about the Church or our doctrines.

These people need us, and we should not, like the Levite, pass by on the other side with a contemptuous sniff because, on this point or that, their approach differs from our own. Our Lord said, 'Go out all over the world and preach the Gospel to the whole of creation.' There is no record that He added, 'But be careful not to associate with people whose theology is inexact.'

'The Realisation of a Common Peril'

That co-operation between Christians is desirable is the clear teaching of the present Pope, but such co-operation except in purely secular activities is not easy. It is not surprising that many Christians outside the visible unity of the Church should resent our claim that the Church is unique, that there can be no question of the reunion of that which has never been divided, and that the problem to be solved is how best to persuade communions which have gone into schism to return to the unity of the undivided Church. Though the logic of our position demands such clarification it is only to be expected that our claims should so often provoke resentment. It is, indeed, difficult for the Church not to give offence by declining to send representatives to conferences where their presence might be interpreted as conceding that the membership of the Catholic Church is not confined to those in visible communion with Rome.

Catholics cannot reasonably be expected to compliment away their own position in the interests of charity. None the less,

there was never a time when co-operation between Christians
of different communions was more important than it is today,
and if Catholics have to withdraw from M.R.A. it is difficult
to envisage conditions under which Catholics could co-operate
with other Christians, excepting of course as citizens in secular
activities, for at Caux every condition for co-operation on
which we could reasonably insist has been conceded.

I have attended many of the Reunion Conferences convened
by my father, and nowhere except at Caux have I found a
complete absence of hostility to and great reverence for the
Catholic Church. A Benedictine priest at Caux commented to
me on the friendliness of all MRAs: 'I have,' he said, 'been
deeply edified by the attitude of these people. They have had
little but rebuffs from us and in some cases they have been
the target of intemperate and uncharitable attack, but their
attitude of respect for the Church and of friendliness for
Catholics has never been affected.'

The prejudice against M.R.A. is based on certain misconceptions: (1) That M.R.A. is an organisation and as such a
rival to the Church. M.R.A. is a spiritual discipline warmly
recommended by many Catholic priests. M.R.A. is a religious
discipline but it is NOT a religion. (2) That M.R.A. leads to
indifferentism.

That it does not lead to indifferentism but to a great deepen-
ing of Catholic life is the conviction of every priest at Caux
with whom I have discussed Moral Re-Armament. How could
a movement which insists on absolute standards awaken in the
mind of a Catholic the suspicion that the teachings of the
Catholic Church were only relatively true? The emphasis on
the absolute is in itself an insurance against indifferentism.

Neither U.N.O., nor the political parties which are described
as Christian, nor Socialism, have the slightest hope of reunit-
ing the threatened West. The roots of Europe are still Christian, and the only hope is the co-operation of all Christians
and the determination to translate what we believe into practice. Such co-operation so far from involving the slightest doctrinal concessions by the Church would, I am convinced, be
the first step to the 'Great Return' of those who have left the
unity of the Church.

Further, this very purpose of a revolutionary unity of the moral forces under God is the thing for which the Pope has repeatedly called and which we have conspicuously failed to create.

To sum up. In my many visits to Caux I have been impressed not so much by the public presentation but by the lives of the M.R.A. workers. I found men practising the economics of Christ, acting with heroic confidence on the belief that the money for their bare necessities would somehow turn up. I found rich men putting into practice that Catholic teaching on wealth which the Middle Ages insisted on more than we do today, that the rich man is only the trustee of such wealth as he possesses. I found married couples whose conception of marital relations is more austere than ours, perhaps too austere.

I could find neither in their speeches, their writings, nor their private conversations anything but genuine reverence for the Catholic Church.

We Catholics have many declared enemies, and many who call themselves Christians who can be relied on to support our persecutors in Spain yesterday or East of the Iron Curtain today.

Is it wise—I will not ask is it generous—to attribute discreditable motives to those whose every action and every pronouncement is either friendly to us or consistent with their professions of friendship?

In 1938, when the civil war in Spain was still raging, my father, Sir Henry Lunn, a Methodist, successfully moved an amendment to a resolution at the Methodist Conference calling for sympathy with Niemöller and the persecuted Christians in Spain. In reply to a letter which Sir Henry wrote in *The Times*, Cardinal Hinsley wrote:

> Those who belong to the Catholic and Roman Church will have read with appreciation and respect Sir Henry Lunn's moving appeal in your columns for a united Christian Front against the world-wide anti-Christian onslaught. Pius XI explicitly appeals in his letter *Divini Redemptoris* to all who believe in God. Between those who believe in Christ as true God and true Man and worship Him, there should be charity—an effort to draw nearer

to Him and so nearer to one another. This means not only friendly relationship but mutual help in defending the civilisation which is founded on the truths enunciated in the Nicene Creed. Sir Henry rightly insists on this bond between us. Let us be frank. There have been in the past misunderstandings and faults of manner on both sides, and of temper and lack of charity in controversy. These, our failings and differences, the enemies of religion have exploited. But the realisation of a common peril is drawing Christians together in practical sympathy.

There is today far more cause for alarm than in 1938. Soviet Russia, which was foiled in the attempt to capture Spain, has since taken over about a third of non-Russian Europe, and has extended the rule of the hammer and sickle over China, North Korea and the greater part of Indo-China. It was important, as the Cardinal insisted, for Catholics in 1938 to co-operate in what he described as 'a united Christian Front against a world-wide anti-Christian onslaught'. It is incomparably more important today.

Postscript (21st September 1956)

The last section is almost identical with the letter with which *The Tablet* correspondence on M.R.A. was concluded, and it would have been open to those who disagreed with me to reply that I had overlooked the distinction between a Catholic group, organised as such, co-operating with Protestants, and Catholics forming part of a non-Catholic group.

Most of the objections to Catholic participation would be removed if the Catholics in M.R.A. did form a definite group who met at regular intervals to discuss how best they could help their non-Catholic friends in M.R.A. to find the truth. At Caux, of course, they would meet under the chairmanship of the priest appointed by the Bishop of the diocese to look after their spiritual needs. Catholics in M.R.A. should, and indeed do regard M.R.A. as a field for missionary activity and not as the final solution to the problems of this distracted planet.

Many Catholics in M.R.A. are doing what they can to enlarge the horizons of their non-Catholic friends in the movement. The ambitions of one such Catholic in M.R.A. was summed up by a Presbyterian as 'To help Catholics outside of M.R.A. to a better understanding of M.R.A. and to help Protestants in M.R.A. to a better understanding of Catholicism.' If Catholics continue to play a part in M.R.A. they should redouble their efforts to influence the movement. They could profitably co-operate with such Anglicans in the movement who are interested in theology and who are familiar with the classics of Anglican scholarship. Professor C. S. Lewis's books, if more widely read, would have a salutary influence on M.R.A.

I fully realise that it will be very difficult to establish such a Concordat, for M.R.A. naturally dislike the prospect of the creation of a Catholic Cell, specially designed to influence M.R.A. in the direction of the Church, but unless the Catholics are organised in a separate group I fear that Catholic participation in M.R.A. may in the near future be forbidden. It is the fear of such a veto which is, I am convinced, holding back many MRAs from submitting to the Church, as indeed is clear from a statement submitted to me by Mr. Andrew Strang with which I will bring this chapter to a close:

Statement by Mr. W. Andrew Strang

Having been brought up in a rather narrow evangelical circle of Scottish Presbyterianism, I was filled with prejudices against the Catholic Church. After I met Moral Re-Armament and began to work with Dr. Buchman, I was astonished to meet Catholics at meetings and house parties. At that time my reaction was to thank God for so many 'brands plucked from the burning'. But I still avoided them, especially as all of them said that meeting Moral Re-Armament had made them better Catholics.

During the war I met a number of priests, clerical brothers and lay brothers in German prison camps, whose caring and interest in raising the morale of the camps were identical to mine. This drew us very close together as we gave ourselves to meet the needs of men in difficulties. Through this I lost all my prejudices and became deeply interested in Catholicism.

After the war my interest increased as my Catholic friends in M.R.A., with great sympathy and understanding, began to introduce me to the truths of Catholicism. I was presented with a Rosary which was blessed by the Pope and also a Missal which I study regularly and use when I have slipped into Mass at

St. Peter's, Rome, and on many other occasions in different countries.

Over the postwar years I have built up a library of books that have helped me enormously. I have St. Thomas Aquinas's *Summa* and a most helpful four-volume treatise on it, St. Augustine's writings, all the biographies I can find on St. Francis of Assisi, all Thomas Merton's books including *Seeds of Contemplation* which I read daily for long periods. I also have Thomas à Kempis' *Imitation of Christ* which I carry with me always, Brother Lawrence's *Practising the Presence of God*, and *The Little Flowers of St. Francis*, all of which I use in my hour's meditation early each morning. Other books I have read time and again are St. Francis de Salles's *Introduction to a Life of Devotion* and the writings of St. John of the Cross and St. Bernard of Clairvaux.

In giving all my time voluntarily to the work of Moral Re-Armament in Africa over the last nine years, some of my best friends have been Catholics, including the late Father Conneny, a professor at the Seminary in Pretoria. Another has been a member of the Third Order of St. Francis.

Unfortunately, in certain places and at certain times, our Catholic colleagues and friends have come under prohibitions. The uncertainty created by this has frequently had a damaging effect on the progress of winning revolutionary and Communistic figures in critical situations in Africa, and has sometimes even prevented lapsed Catholics from returning to the Church. It has also turned many who were coming close to the Church from going any further.

XV

THE M.R.A. WORLD OUTLOOK

IN the course of a broadcast (4th June 1956) Dr. Buchman said, 'Nations without an ideology are being out-thought by those with one.'

The underlying implication of M.R.A. propaganda is that Russia has an ideology and that England and other Western countries have none. If an ideology be defined as a faith for which men are prepared to die, the faith which saved England in 1940 was certainly an ideology. England in 1940 was far more united than Russia in 1941. Had the Nazis invaded England, few indeed would have been the Quislings to welcome them, but Hitler's armies were welcomed with flowers in the Ukraine as liberators from an odious tyranny. It was only Hitler's insensate folly in allowing Rosenberg to treat the conquered Ukrainians as helots which unified Russia against him. Even so, thousands of White Russians fought in his ranks.

We now know from Khrushchev's revelations that the ruling class in Russia were held together less by a common ideology than by a common funk. Stalin, we are now assured, was alone responsible for the blockade of Berlin in 1949, for the war in Korea, and for the arbitrary arrest and assassination of thousands of innocent victims. Once when Khrushchev was addressing a crowded audience on the evils of Stalinism, a voice from the back of the hall was heard to say, 'Why then did you do nothing about it?'

'Will the Comrade who asked that question,' said Khrushchev, stand up?' Nobody stood up. 'Now you know,' said Khrushchev, 'why we did nothing about it.' Common funk is still the great bond of unity in Russia.

There is no common ideology in Russia. The underground

Church is increasingly active. A Russian priest whom I met in Switzerland, and who was returning to Russia, told me that many Russians, nominally Communists, have their children baptised in secret, and that Russians who are married by the State will often send their rings to a priest, who places them on the altar and reads the marriage service. We know that the intellectuals are in a state of latent revolt, and that the more intelligent of the younger generation are increasingly dissatisfied by Marxism.

'Frank Buchman,' Francis Goulding said to me, 'has never maintained that all Russians are united by a common ideology. His argument is that here is a country effectively controlled by 3 per cent of the population who are planning evil. If, then, England were controlled by a 3 per cent minority of God-guided men, our major problems would be solved.'

Maybe, but Dr. Buchman does not explain the steps by which this minority can achieve and retain control of a democratic country.

God endowed man with the dignity of free will, and the price to be paid for that dignity is the freedom to choose error. Man is free to reject Christ and His Church. The West is free and *therefore* disunited. Russia is enslaved and superficially united—by terror.

The broadcast from which I have just quoted contains a sentence on which I commented earlier in this book: 'The new alignment in the world is between nations who think and nations who do not think.' I am unable to interpret this cryptic utterance and perhaps for that very reason suspect that a more important distinction, to which Dr. Buchman might devote some attention, is between dictatorships and democracies. A dictator can impose his foreign policy, a democratic government is impotent to impose a sound policy against the will of the electorate. It was the self-indulgent pacifism of Demos which imposed the policy of appeasement on a Tory Government. There are times, as Spengler remarks, when the effective choice is not between war and peace but between victory and defeat, and to victory belongs the price of victory. And this is a price which Demos is unwilling to pay until faced,

as we were in 1940, with destruction. It is the weakness of
democracy that the politician who offers bribes will usually
defeat the politician who demands sacrifices.

Though the M.R.A. analysis of the continuing successes
of militant Communism seems to me to suffer from over-
simplification, I hope that the influence of M.R.A. will continue to increase because they are more awake than most of
our countrymen to the diabolical ingenuity of Communist
methods of infiltration, and have been remarkably successful
in changing Communists. I could wish, however, that the
word 'apostasy' was as often on their lips as the word 'ideology': for apostasy is the key to the world situation. National
disaster has always in the past been the fate of apostate nations.
The German State, though not the German people, apo-
statised under Hitler, and the Babylonian captivity of Eastern
Germany is the price that they are paying, as did the Israelites
of old, for whoring after strange gods. It will be our turn next
if the advance of secularism be not checked.

M.R.A. may be over-sanguine and too *simpliste*, but in spite
of certain misconceptions their world outlook seems to be
sound. They are surely right to insist on the dangers that
threaten us and no less right to hope that the world may yet
be saved. Hilaire Belloc considered that the most marked
characteristic of the modern world was 'a rising tide of despair'.
With this diagnosis few people in M.R.A. would be disposed
to disagree, but they are no less convinced that they have a
sovereign cure for despair.

Secularism has already eroded the great culture of the West.
The structure still stands, but it is difficult not to be infected
by the pessimism of Leopardi as he gazed on the walls and
arches and columns which we have inherited from the past,
but could see no traces of the departed glory. The decline of
morals is more responsible than any other single factor for
'the rising tide of despair'.

> *vedo le mura e gli archi*
> *E la colonne e i simulacri a l'erme . . .*
> *Ma la gloria non vedo*

The contrast between modern England and the Victorian

England in which I was born emphasises the importance of continuing to preach what many of us have great difficulty in practising. The Victorian age accepted as self-evident the Christian moral code, but admitted that it was easier to preach this code than to practise it. Modern Europe speaks with confused voices on these basic issues. In Sweden, it would seem the code has been semi-officially abandoned. Joe David Brown created a sensation by his article in *Time* (25th April 1955) entitled 'Sin and Sweden'. He interviewed a lady officially appointed by the Government to teach sex in the schools.

'I tell the girls,' said this Government servant, 'that it is all right to sleep with a boy, but first they must be in love. When I tell them that you see them smiling and nudging each other.'

There is always a lag between preaching and practice, and the lag would seem to be constant. When the Christian sex code was preached there was a big gap between the code which was officially acknowledged and the practice of the average citizen. Today where immorality is preached by many in responsible positions the average standard of sexual behaviour is far lower than it was in the last century. When I was young it was wholly exceptional for a girl in the middle or upper classes to have an affair before marriage. Now it is far from exceptional. The great psychologist Jung is not a Christian, but he writes that Christianity was accepted 'to escape at last from the brutality of antiquity. . . .'

As soon as we discard it, [writes Jung] licentiousness returns. The meaning of Christianity and Mithraism is clear. It is a moral restraint of animal impulses. The dynamic of both religions betrays something of that enormous feeling of redemption which animated the first disciples and which we today scarcely know how to appreciate. Those old truths are empty to us. Most certainly we should still understand them had our customs even a breath of the ancient brutality, for we can hardly realise in this day the whirlwinds of unchained libido which roared through the ancient Rome of the Caesars.

'And what,' I asked, 'attracted you to M.R.A.?' My friend

M

Hannen Foss, with whom I had many stimulating talks at Caux, paused for a moment and replied, 'Hope . . . M.R.A. offered hope instead of despair.'

M.R.A. offers men liberation, liberation from the 'unchained libido'. I remember an Asiatic who had met M.R.A. in London. 'For three months after I met M.R.A. I never had an impure thought, and when they returned I could cope with them. I walked on air. I can't describe the sense of liberation.' Hope of self-conquest, hope of changing others through self-change, hope that a new renaissance has dawned . . . such is the basis of the M.R.A. World Outlook.

One evening after an M.R.A. play I got into conversation with the lady who was pouring out tea, Miss Kirstie Morrison of St. Anne's College, Oxford, and one of the earliest members of the Oxford Group.

'The trouble,' she said, 'with most of us in the educated classes is that we're complaisant about ourselves, and cynical about God and His power to change the world if we co-operate. The idiom of our little world will soon be a dead language, but we still think in terms of those pleasant little cultural holidays in Italy and Spain or France. Meanwhile the world moves towards catastrophe.' And as she spoke I remembered Pascal's '*Nous courons sans souci dans le précipice, après que nous avons mis quelque chose devant nous pour nous empêcher de le voir.*'

The MRAs' world outlook is well informed and realistic. They have world-wide sources of information, for their teams are working in most countries. They know that many of the most effective Communists in high places are described as social democrats, and they fully realise that the only thing which prevents Russia taking over Sweden, Norway and Denmark is the fear of a world war.

Auge Andersen whom I met at Caux, is a Norwegian just like many another Norwegian whom I have met in the skiing world. He was not exactly cheerful about Norway or about the influence and posthumous influence of the eminent Communist, Erling K. Falk, who founded the *Mot Dag* (Towards the Day) movement in the late 'twenties and who had such a pernicious influence on the University of Oslo and on the young men who could not resist his sinister charm, and who became his devoted disciples. 'Some of his disciples,' said Andersen, 'are in key positions today. Of course, they do not call themselves Communists.'

Andersen was with the M.R.A. cast that played *The Forgotten Factor* in Mo I Rana, a northern town in which there is an important steel works. The workers and the shop-stewards came to the play and the Communist Chairman dropped ten kroner into the plate where contributions towards expenses— there was no charge for admission—were gratefully received.

Before M.R.A. came to Mo I Rana the Communists held ten seats out of fifteen in the Trade Union Executive. Three weeks after the visit of M.R.A. the Communist representation sank to two seats. The President and Vice-President of the Union are committed to M.R.A.

Catholicism in Scandinavia is very weak. I have lectured to the Catholics in Oslo and in Copenhagen (where, by the way, a lecture described by me as 'Europe from a Catholic Angle' was announced on a notice outside the hall as 'Europe by a Catholic Angel'), and I admit sadly that it is difficult to overcome the inherited prejudice of the Scandinavians against the Catholic Church. Certainly Catholic influence on Communism in Scandinavia is for the moment unimportant.

In the course of *The Forgotten Factor* tour the student president at one of the universities visited in Scandinavia spent an evening with the team after the performance in the theatre. 'What we really need,' he said to Andersen, 'is to get rid of the sense of guilt. I do not believe in "absolute purity", but one thing puzzles me about you people. You all look so happy, and I must admit that I'm a frustrated man.'

Whilst on the subject of drama, something should be said of Peter Howard's work. The typescript as originally submitted to the publishers included a chapter on the M.R.A. plays. As the book was too long this chapter had to be dropped, but it is important to insist that Howard's *The Real News* in which he makes good use of his experience as a journalist is in quite a different class to *The Vanishing Island*. The characterisation is excellent, and there is plenty of humour in the play. The most famous and most successful of the M.R.A. plays is *The*

Forgotten Factor, by Alan Thornhill, an outstanding performance. This and the Finnish cinema play, *The Answer,* are my favourites. Sibelius thought so well of this latter play that he broke the rule of a lifetime and wrote the music for it, the first film play which he has thus honoured.

XVI

SUMMING UP

THE criticisms of M.R.A. which are to be found in this book are all variants on the same theme—the argument from proportion. I miss in M.R.A. what I find in the Catholic Church, balance and proportion. I can best explain what I mean by a long quotation from Hilaire Belloc.

And here to end up with, [writes Belloc] is another minor argument which will appeal less perhaps to others than it does to me. It appeals to me strongly because I feel it in every line of good verse, in every excellent room or monument, in every phrase of good music, in every admirable character; I mean the argument from Proportion. Nowhere else, in all the experience of mankind, will you discover universal Proportion as you discover it in the doctrine of the Catholic Church. Though it applies to the whole of human life, it does, in every relation, keep the normal—which some have translated 'the Mean'. It does so in the relations of parent and child, of husband and wife, of the propertied man and the destitute, of the citizen and the Christian (I mean of our duty to the Prince and our duty to God). It does so in that most difficult of all actual problems, the management of appetite. . . .

Men have achieved proportion outside the Faith in one department at the expense of another. They have had the grace given them to satisfy the human spirit to the full in column and arch—and meanwhile despised beauty. They have had a just arrangement of property, and meanwhile have lost culture. But in the Catholic scheme there inhabits a certain balancing compensating spirit, which though it can never constrain men to achieve perfect proportion, for men have fallen, does make them approach to such perfection sufficiently for the right conduct of life.

The dissuasions which have made it difficult for me to do full justice to M.R.A. are all variants of one major dissuasion.

I miss in M.R.A. 'a certain balancing compensating spirit' which is native to the Catholic climate, though often lacking in individual Catholics, a compensating spirit which serves as a check on that tendency to over simplification which is one of the great weaknesses of M.R.A. I need not repeat the illustrations cited in earlier chapters to support this criticism.

I miss this 'balancing spirit' not only in M.R.A. but also in most criticisms of M.R.A. Just as the more violent Protestant criticisms of the Church often attempt to prove themselves impartial by admitting that there are men with a sincere devotion to our Lord even in the 'Roman Church', men who are saintly in spite of rather than because of their membership of the Catholic Church, so there are Catholics who after a perfunctory reference to the heroic self-sacrifice of the full-time workers, summarise every point that could possibly be made against M.R.A. In a pamphlet of this kind the important fact that many lapsed Catholics have returned to the Church as the result of their contact with M.R.A. was relegated to a footnote.

There are many reasons why it is not easy to be just to M.R.A. Indeed, many critics of M.R.A. remind me of what Tertullian said of the enemies of Christianity: *"Ideo et credunt de nobis quae non probantur, et nolunt inquiri ne probentur non esse quae malunt."*[1]

It is difficult to be just to M.R.A. because all one's snobbish instincts conspire to persuade one to dissociate oneself from a movement which is so unfashionable and which does so little to conciliate the aesthetic prejudices of the educated classes. Fashion is a tawdry but a powerful ally of all critics of M.R.A.

M.R.A. propaganda in general and their terminology in particular are a gift to the satirist. *Haec et nos risimus aliquando,* if I may make my own Tertullian's confession that he too had been among the scoffers of Christianity.

A critic of M.R.A. who is less anxious to make out a case than to discover the truth will not dismiss in a few words or sentences the quality of life produced by M.R.A. He will not

---

[1] Thus they both believe things about us which are not proved, and are unwilling to inquire lest that should be disproved which they prefer to believe, *Ap.* ii. 19.

content himself with a perfunctory tribute to men, many of whom have abandoned careers in which they had every hope of great success, for an unsalaried position in a movement which most of their former colleagues regard with a mixture of disdain and hostility. On the contrary, he will translate what they have done into what he would have to do if he followed their example. I, for instance, felt differently about some of these men when I forced myself to realise that their sacrifice was comparable to that which I should have made if I had adopted a way of life which kept me permanently below the Alpine snowline, cut me off from writing, and made it impossible for me to influence the development of ski-ing. Peter Howard had made a brilliant start as a journalist, one of Lord Beaverbrook's protégés; Morris Martin was the youngest Doctor of Philosophy in Oxford with every prospect of a distinguished academic career; Alan Thornhill was a Fellow of Hertford College, Oxford; Paul Campbell an intensely ambitious and successful young doctor, and these are only a few of the many full-time workers who had made a mark in their particular callings when they turned their back on success, as this world counts success.

M.R.A. demands from the full-time workers not only the sacrifice of a career but also the sacrifice of pride. It is not easy for a proud man to live on gifts, particularly if he be married. In an earlier chapter I had insisted that Peter Howard could quote what seemed to be exaggerated tributes to his play *The Vanishing Island* without weakening my conviction that he was essentially humble, and I found the clue to this enigma in a book, which I read after I wrote that chapter, Father James Broderick's admirable study of Saint Ignatius Loyola.

> After an agonising struggle, [writes Father Broderick] he broke, with God's grace, the subtle pervasive power of vanity in his soul so completely that he could tell how brave he had been at Pamplona and what magnificent fortitude he had shown in his subsequent sufferings, without the slightest tremor of self-satisfaction. These good qualities were no less the gift of God than the supernatural grace which enabled him to see them as such and to refer the glory to where it alone belonged.

Nobody could live for some weeks with these men without

being deeply impressed by the shattering conviction with which they acted on the principle that 'where God guides He provides'. The serenity of these people under conditions which would drive me sick with anxiety is very edifying. Let me repeat what I have already said more than once, that nobody in M.R.A. claims that they are the first to live or to travel by faith. All they do claim is to have put into practice an old principle which has never failed.

I was reminded of many of these M.R.A. journeys, planned before anybody had a clue as to whence the necessary money was coming, when I read of St. Ignatius' pilgrimage to the Holy Land. He had no money for the journey to Jerusalem, and 'many were the arguments advanced that it was impossible to get a passage without paying for it, but in his own soul he was certain beyond all doubt that he would find a way'. When the kindly people who had tried to dissuade him from attempting the pilgrimage failed to move him they gave him six or seven ducats towards the price of his passage. He accepted these reluctantly and began to feel that he had shown a lack of confidence in God and eventually distributed them among the poor men he met on the way to Venice. The surprising series of apparent accidents which enabled him to finance his passage to and from Palestine described in Father Broderick's book, conform to a pattern which is familiar to those who have been curious enough to investigate the finances of M.R.A. missions.

Before I became a Catholic I spent some time investigating the claims of Spiritualism, and came to the conclusion that some of the phenomena were supernormal, but whatever discarnate intelligences were responsible, these intelligences were certainly not the departed dead. The reality of praeternatural phenomena is in itself no evidence of divine agency. Many of the phenomena which we associate with saints, such as stigmata, have been duplicated by those who have not the slightest claim to sanctity. Ultimately it is the quality of life which is the criterion for distinguishing between the supernatural and the praeternatural. Nobody who has taken the trouble, as I have, to investigate the private finances of MRAs living on faith could resist the conclusion that there was no purely natural explanation of the unending succession of providential interventions which saved either individuals or teams from dire financial calamity. These interventions are either divine or diabolic, and between these alternatives let the reader choose for himself without any prompting from me.

I remember a long talk at Caux with a priest who was highly critical, indeed almost unfriendly. I raised the question of this financing by faith. 'What is your view?' I asked. 'Do you believe that whatever mistakes M.R.A. may have made, God is behind it?' 'Sans doute,' he replied.

From the premise that God is working through M.R.A. I do not draw the conclusion that it is impious to criticise it, but I do feel that criticisms should be tempered by charity and by sympathy. Nothing is easier than to sneer at M.R.A. But for my own part when I find men and women who have sacrificed everything to conform to God's will I will do what I can to ensure that the sneer and the snigger are excluded from anything which I write or say on this subject.

Many full-time workers have sacrificed the hope of a distinguished career; all have sacrificed the income which they would have been otherwise earning.

Nothing but the conviction of a supernatural mission could keep them faithful to their vocation. Friends of mine, with whom I have discussed M.R.A., have been quick to point out what I have not been in the least disposed to deny, that there are far more austere vocations than that of M.R.A., the Trappists, for instance. Some of those who make such comparisons remind me of the tourist who refused to look at Mont Blanc because it was not as high as Everest.

Many people would find it easier to sacrifice career and income than to sacrifice their privacy. These men and women of M.R.A. begin their day with an hour of meditation at 6 a.m. (Quiet Time), and till the last cup of tea after the play at about 11 p.m. they are at the disposal of their fellow men. They are giving out the whole time, and, what is more, they are always cheerful and good tempered. The MRAs must find it difficult to resist boredom, but they show no sign of being bored. There is inevitably a tremendous sameness about the speeches at the Assemblies. A speaker who has just been changed may find his own experience and his own speech new and exciting, but few of them strike a note which the full-time workers have not heard scores or hundreds of times. *Man muss das Wahre immer wiederholen.* Of course Goethe was right, one must keep on repeating the truth, but from what I know of Goethe I am sure that he would have found it far easier to keep on repeating than to keep on listening to other people repeating the truth.

Requiem at Dellwood

During a long week-end in the M.R.A. headquarters at Dellwood near New York, we heard that Mrs. Hofmeyr's father and step-mother had been murdered by the Mau Mau.

Bremer Hofmeyr belongs to one of the leading political families of South Africa. His family have held five senior Cabinet posts in the South African Government. It was at Oxford, where Bremer Hofmeyr narrowly missed a Blue for rugby, that he first met M.R.A. and sacrificed the certainty of a distinguished career to give his life to the movement.

His wife, Agnes Leakey, belongs to one of the great pioneering families in Kenya. In the Second World War her eldest brother was awarded the V.C. The next brother was awarded both the D.S.O. and M.C.

The last time that Mrs. Hofmeyr saw her father, who had become a supporter of M.R.A., she tried hard to persuade him and his wife to come and stay with her in South Africa. They refused. 'Our place is with the loyal Africans. We can carry firearms but the Africans can't, and if we leave they will probably be killed. Whatever happens we believe that what we are doing is right,' and they added that if the Mau Mau came to the farm they were ready to die if that was what God wanted. They only prayed that if death came it would be quick. This prayer was not granted. Death when it came was not quick, at least for Gray Leakey. His wife and servant were murdered quickly enough, but he was buried alive.

'It gave me,' said Mrs. Hofmeyr, 'tremendous courage to see their lack of fear of whatever would happen. We all had a sense that we might not meet again.'

And as she spoke I remembered Regulus calmly saying

farewell to his family before returning to Carthage—to torture and to death. And across the bridge of time I heard the Horatian lines which are as true of Gray Leakey as of Regulus.

atqui sciebat quis sibi barbarus
Tortor pararet

'Although he knew', or perhaps it would be truer to say, 'although he guessed what the barbarian torturer was preparing for him', Leakey stayed at his post and said farewell to his daughter with Roman *gravitas*.

On that Sunday at Dellwood we met to do honour to those who had died at their post. 'For my stepmother,' said Mrs. Hofmeyr, 'it was a speedy going. For my father I don't know. Yesterday there were two thousand people searching for his body.'

Many years ago a great friend of mine, Dick Waghorn, Schneider Trophy winner, was killed flying a few hours before the annual dinner of the Ski Club of Great Britain. As President I had to refer to his death. I was very fond of Dick, and I remember how difficult I found it to control my voice. Mrs. Hofmeyr spoke without a tremor though the possibility that her father had died a terrible death was ever present to her mind.

M.R.A. and This Book

There is a letter of Cicero's in which he suggests to his friend Lucceius, an historical writer, that the story of Cicero's consulship might provide Lucceius with an excellent subject for a book. 'I earnestly ask you,' wrote Cicero, 'in consideration of our friendship, to credit me with a little more than would be allowed by Truth.'

No such suggestions were made to me by my friends at Caux who read *Enigma* in typescript. As I have suggested that MRAs as a whole are unduly sensitive to critics, it is only fair to add that their comments were confined to minor misstatements which I have corrected, and they were good enough to say that they had found the book readable.

I enjoyed the talks provoked by my typescript. 'I often squirmed on the World Mission,' said General Channer, 'while

Howard was apologising for the British, but I must admit that when I was serving in India my own attitude was one of unconscious superiority.'

A. L.: I wonder whether it wasn't merely a legitimate pride. There is nothing wrong in that. When the Chief Captain admitted that he had paid a great price to obtain the freedom of Roman citizenship, St. Paul, you remember, replied, 'But I was born free,' and down the ages one can still hear the ring of pride in his voice. Why should we be ashamed of our citizenship of an empire with as great a record as the Roman?

General Channer: I'm not in the least ashamed of that, but I do feel apologetic for making other people feel small. I was explaining this to an Indian judge with whom I was staying when the World Mission was in India. He said that there were many things for which India could be grateful to the British—the legal system, for instance.

A. L.: And he is not unique. There is a great deal of friendliness for us, mixed with resentment and hostility for which a minority of our people must certainly be blamed, but as Francis Goulding said, it was in the main a minority. Many Englishmen in India went out of their way to understand the people among whom they were living and to cultivate personal relations.

A very fine African, whose name I think was Thoma, paid a memorable tribute on the platform at Caux to the services which England had rendered to Africa, and it is argued that this tribute proves the usefulness of the reiterated apologies to the Asiatics and Africans. But M.R.A. has got to win the British, not only the Africans, and it is a pity that those who insist that they are neither anti-Communist nor anti-Capitalist should provide their critics with the opportunity to describe them as anti-British, which they certainly are not.

This constant sniping at our record in the East may be intended to provoke contrition. Its only effect on me was to provoke me into my first serious attempt to defend our Imperial record. It would, I am convinced, be far better if M.R.A. never discussed either the services which our country has rendered to Africa and Asia or the grievances of Asiatics and

Africans. We have given India independence and Africa self-government, and our objective henceforward should be to co-operate in the future rather than to continue to dwell in the past.

One of my motives for writing this book is to diminish the prejudice against M.R.A. in England, but the MRAs must co-operate by reconsidering some of their less prudent lines of propaganda. An MRA, who was a great admirer of Sir Arthur Bryant, wondered wistfully whether Sir Arthur could ever be lured to Caux. I should not like him to be present when apologies were being freely offered for the British Empire. He would not like this sort of thing at all.

Here is a quotation from one of his articles in *The Illustrated London News* (9th June 1956):

There was just as much tendency in the nineteenth century as there is today for ambitious tyrants, nationalistic passions and rivalries and mob hysteria to threaten the peace of the Orient, the Middle East and Africa, and the forgotten names of a whole succession of warlike and megalomaniac Egyptians, Chinese, Burmese, Afghan, Persian, Abyssinian, Swazi, Gold Coast, Zulu, Matabele and Sudanese petty tyrants and fanatics are reminders of the fact. The only reason why they can now be described as petty tyrants, and that their names and exploits are forgotten, is that the conflagrations they lit were fought and extinguished before they had become too great for the peace of mankind by the British-Indian Army transported and supported by the Royal Navy. All the loose talk and thinking, so prevalent and popular today, about the evils of colonisation, overlook this elementary historical fact. The British Empire—I use the word to distinguish it from the Commonwealth—during its comparatively short existence, for it only operated effectively in this way for just over one hundred years, was principally a police system for preserving peace over a large area of the globe. Whatever may be said about that Empire's other achievements or lack of achievements, it was by far the most peaceful century in human annals.

I hope I have not left in the mind of the reader the impression that I am blind to the defects of our record. Any tendency, however, I might have to undue complacency about our role in Africa would have been checked on reading page 33 of

African Wonderland, by James Riddell. Riddell, a former vice-captain of our ski team, is a brilliant writer, and his balanced attitude to what is called the native problem is effective precisely because it is balanced.

The last thing I desire is to underestimate the magnificent work which M.R.A. is doing in improving inter-racial relations, but I am convinced that the good results so far achieved are due far more to the positive aspect of M.R.A., the affection which they have lavished on the Africans, their quiet and persistent work in eroding racial barriers, than to the negative aspect, sniping at the British. It is in Africa that their most effective work is being done, and as a pendant to the tribute which *The Times* paid to their work in Nigeria, I reproduce a few paragraphs from a Nigerian paper owned and edited by Africans, *The Eastern Sentinal Enugu*, February 1956:

> The Play (*Freedom*) deals with the basic issue—not the attainment of self-government which for us is assured, but the quality of self-government that is to be practised. For the men of M.R.A. are pioneers of a new battle which has to be won—the battle for unity, honesty in public and private life and democracy based on absolute moral standards.
>
> We consider the timing of the play to be JUST RIGHT for this year, 1956, is Nigeria's year of destiny. The visit of Her Majesty the Queen and the Duke of Edinburgh has focused the attention of the country on the need for maintaining the national unity which the Royal Couple's visit has occasioned. We believe this Force can fulfil it.
>
> Many of our leaders from all parts of Nigeria owe much to Caux for the influence of M.R.A. since 1949 has been greater than anyone can assess. It has produced stability in this country without which the Queen's visit would not have happened. We believe the play *Freedom* can make permanent the spirit of unity we are enjoying at the moment. The coming of the play *Freedom* at just this point is extremely appropriate.

Big and Little Fishes

'I should never,' said the late Cardinal Hinsley to me, 'use the word heretic in connection with a good and devout Christian such as your father, for the word implies the wilful rejection of truth.' M.R.A., as I have already suggested, is a *hairesis* rather than a heresy, but it seems to me to fulfil that function for which, so St. Augustine believed, heresy is permitted. 'Heretics,' he said, 'are given us that we should not remain in infancy.'

It was, I think, the Dean of Strasbourg who said that though Catholicism had nothing to learn from M.R.A., many Catholics had a great deal to learn. I can only speak for myself with certainty, and I know what I learned at Caux, a new emphasis on the old truth that every Christian should be a fisher of men. Admittedly I have been quite successful in creating a fisher-man façade. I enjoyed my published controversies with Coulton and Haldane and Joad, and if anybody starts up an argument about Catholicism in my presence I will join in with gusto, but I acquiesce in the convention that it is bad form to force our religious views on other people. I am always meeting non-Christians, slack Christians and fallen away Christians, and I find it on the whole far more comfortable to discuss politics or ski-ing or literature than to make the slightest effort to 'change' them. And, of course, I have no difficulty in rationalising what is in fact a concession to fashion. I know all the soothing formulae. 'You do no good by forcing your beliefs on other people. . . . Wait until you're given an opening, etc., etc.'

MRAs have forced themselves to overcome this natural dif-fidence. They believe that they can render no greater service to their fellow men than awakening in them that appetite for God of which St. Augustine speaks—'Thou hast made us for Thyself and our souls shall not find rest until they rest in Thee.' There is far too little of that spirit in modern Christianity, Catholic or Protestant. Pelagius was right. *Si volumus non redire currendum est*, which may be loosely rendered, 'If the Church militant does not take the offensive, it is doomed to retreat.'

How is it that Peter Howard can write a play and an M.R.A. team, mainly non-Catholics, take that play to an Italian town, largely under Communist influence, and bring back the lead-ing and most influential Communist in the town to the practice of his Faith?

I have already quoted the Catholic chaplain to Basle Uni-versity who asked why he, with all the treasures of the Church to call on, was less successful with his students than these MRAs. To this question there is an answer which is up to a point convincing. The MRAs represent a spiritual élite. It is grossly unfair to Catholicism to compare them with the average Catholic. It would be fairer to compare M.R.A. full-time workers with monks or friars, and MRAs in the world with members of a Third Order.

The main task of the Catholic Church is to get as many souls as possible into purgatory. The Jansenists, like MRAs, aimed at producing an élite, and were contemptuous of those who were not wholly converted. St. Francis de Sales, though full of admiration for the hard life lived by Mother Angélique and her nuns at Port Royal, gently reproved her with that gift, which was also Virgil's, 'for coining a phrase with a meaning far beyond its immediate application'. He said, '*Ma fille, ne vaudrait-il pas mieux ne pas prendre si grands poissons et en prendre davantage.*'

> There will always [as Monsignor Knox remarks[1]] be those who want to draw the meshes tight, so as to bring the little fishes in too, and those who want to leave the meshes wide so that every catch shall be really worth catching. A standard of sanctification which appealed to a few choice souls but left so many others, full of good dispositions, out of the running—could not Mère Angélique be less exacting and cast her nets wider?

The Elder Brother

A German Evangelical whom I met at Caux summed up what he regretted in the attitude of too many Catholics, by a penetrating analogy which Catholics would accept more readily than his own co-religionists. 'It seems to me,' he said, 'that too many of your Catholic theologians concentrate on what M.R.A. is *now*, do not realise that it is changing and cannot make the imaginative effort to realise what it may become. We Evangelicals are like the Prodigal Son in the Parable. We have left our father's house and gone into a far country, but like the Prodigal Son we are on our way home. The Catholic should model himself on the father who saw his son a long way off and ran to meet him, and not on the elder

---

[1] *Enthusiasm*, pp. 46, 210.

brother who stayed at home and sulked and felt he hadn't got the credit he deserved for never having strayed.'

It is not easy for a Catholic to do justice to M.R.A. *Civis Romanus sum.* The old Roman pride has been baptised but not destroyed in the Church of Rome, and it is difficult for the Catholic to believe that any good thing can come out of Caux. I remember my irritation when I found that there were Catholics in M.R.A. who seemed to believe that society could be changed by a movement which lacked the patrimony of doctrine and the supernatural means of grace of the Catholic Church, but when I met these Catholics I soon realised that they did not in point of fact believe that M.R.A. had invented something more effective than the approach of the Catholic Church. What they did believe, and what they were justified in believing, was that M.R.A. could approach within converting distance of many an atheist, Communist or secularist who was too embittered by invincible prejudice to consider the claims of the Catholic Church. Facts are stubborn things, and the facts conclusively prove that many a Communist and many a lapsed Catholic have been brought back to the practice of their religion by M.R.A. MRAs might indeed be compared to irregular units parachuted into enemy territory to work behind the lines until such time as the main army can invade and occupy.

Monsignor Knox somewhere refers contemptuously to what he calls 'the mob loyalties of the Church', the kind of loyalty which sometimes finds consolation for failure to live up to the exacting Catholic standards by contrasting the Church of which one is an unworthy member with other communions.

Now there is, as Archbishop Roberts, S.J., has reminded us, the highest authority for not forbidding those to do good work who are not of our company, but there is no authority for belittling the good works of men and women merely because they do not belong to our communion.

I can understand those who preach class warfare attacking M.R.A., but I am saddened when good Christians are uncharitable in their judgement of those who have proved the sincerity of their devotion to God by heroic sacrifices. MRAs have exaggerated their successes, but surely one need not

N

labour to prove that men and women who systematically work
for the reconciliation of warring elements in industry cannot
fail to have a beneficial influence. Must we really deny the
obvious because the occasional truce they achieve on the industrial battleground owes nothing to us?

MRAs, like the rest of us, are all the more effective for being
criticised, but it is unchristian to dismiss their dedicated lives
with a sneer or a snigger. Their idiom may be unattractive,
but only those who are insensitive to the clear evidence of the
supernatural will fail to temper their criticism with a recognition of the reality which informs this movement. To concentrate on details of presentation and propaganda is to expose
oneself to Pascal's criticism: *C'est une chose monstreuse de voir dans
un même cœur et en même temps cette sensibilité pour les moindres choses
et cette étrange insensibilité pour les plus grandes.*[1] The undoubted
success of M.R.A. illustrates a profound truth.

'The Church rightly maintains,' wrote Dr. Karl Adam, a
professor of Dogmatic Theology, 'and continually reiterates
in decisive and uncompromising fashion, her claim to be
the sole true Body of Christ; but at the same time she holds
a generous and large-minded view regarding the activity of
Christ's grace. That activity has no bonds or limits, but is
as infinite as the love of God. . . . And not merely a Christian
life, but a complete and lofty life, according to the 'full age
of Christ' a saintly life, is possible—so Catholics believe—even
in a definitely non-Catholic Communion.'[2]

It is this same Dr. Adam who published in the Tübingen
Theological Quarterly an article on M.R.A. in the course of
which he wrote:

> Not mere dreamers have followed the movement which within
> thirty years has grown into a great world offensive, but prominent
> intellectuals, world-famous statesmen and politicians, big indus-
> trialists and workers' leaders, trade unionists, dockers and miners,
> men of all conditions from cabinet ministers to cooks. They all
> have one aim, to solve the toughest political, economic, social
> and cultural questions in the light of the Gospel. And it is amaz-
> ing, it is wonderful, how, time after time, it is always the simple,

[1] It is monstrous to see in the same heart and at the same time this sensitiveness
for the unimportant and this insensitivity about the most important things.

[2] *The Spirit of Catholicism* (Revised Edition), pp. 192, 194.

clear concepts of the Sermon on the Mount which throw light
on the most involved political and economic problems. The four
absolutes, the challenge to complete surrender to God, faith in
the power of the Cross of Christ, and the 'quiet time' which
Buchman urges, are basic elements of the Christian life, they are
Christianity lived out. That is why Buchman's message is in its
very core a Christian message.

One can understand why the Catholic finds no new truths in
Caux. But shaken to his roots, he has to admit that in Caux
Christianity has been deeper understood and lived, than in many
Catholic communities. In answer to the question, 'What has
Caux to give Catholics?' Monsignor E. Fischer, Dean of the
Cathedral of Strasbourg, replied, 'The first thing that strikes us
in Caux is the nagging of our conscience. I believe that outside
of the religious orders, there is no place on the face of the earth
where so much prayer goes up.'

N*

XVII

'A LITTLE, WELL-ORDERED CITY'

καὶ τόδε Φωκυλίδεω πόλις σκοπέλῳ κατὰ κόσμον οἰκεσα
σμικρὴ κρέσσων Νίνου ἀραινούσης

ANY a time I have stepped on to my balcony at Caux
and watched the darkness ebb from the steel grey
waters of the eastern lake, and the first rumour of
colour in the open reaches beyond Lausanne. Few views are
lovelier. There is every contrast that one could hope for, the
snows of the Mont Blanc range invading the southern sky, the
Doric splendour of the Dent du Midi, 'Ce Parthenon des Alpes',
the ravines narrow and confined that branch off from the
valley of the Rhone, and the space and freedom of the distant
Jura. And how infinite are the moods of the lake! Pearl grey
in the noontide heat, deep blue when the temperature falls,
dark where the wind ruffles its crystal surface. And how varied
are the patterns etched by moving steamers into its surface,
when ripples woven by the passing craft glitter in the sun like
chain armour.

But it is not only for its beauty that I love this lake; Nazareth
alone among the world's inland seas has greater memories.
From my window I can see Lausanne where Gibbon completed
his *Decline and Fall of the Roman Empire* and strolled through
the acacia-covered avenue reflecting sadly that however long
might be the life and fame of the book, the life of the author
was drawing to its close. It was one of those moments when,
to quote his own words, 'the browner shade which colours the
end of life' was uppermost in his thoughts.

Lausanne recalls Gibbon, Clarens Rousseau, and Montreux
Byron, and Glion just below the terraces of Caux is haunted
by the sad shade of Matthew Arnold. The cone of Jaman rising
above Caux is for ever associated with Arnold.

Ah, Jaman! delicately tall
Above his sun-warmed firs—
What thoughts to me his rocks recall
What memories he stirs.

Memories, in my case, of the poet who wrote these lines.
Arnold first visited Glion in 1846, a century before the terraces of Caux, just above Glion, became the Mecca of a world-
wide movement inspired by a robust faith in those religious
certitudes which Arnold was already mourning as dead. He
loved the poetry of the Faith but was convinced that its doctrines were fast losing their hold on men's minds.

Unduped of fancy, henceforth man
Must labour! must resign
His all too human creeds. . . .

It was at Glion that Arnold wrote this epitaph on Christianity.

It is indeed a strange coincidence that the eastern and
western ends of Lake Leman should have provided headquarters for two great religious movements, Calvinism at
Geneva, M.R.A. at Caux. It was Calvin who made of Geneva
an anti-Rome, a tradition which has survived its creator. It
was at Geneva that Calvin trained the Ironsides of the Re-
formation. It was at Geneva that Rousseau was born, Rousseau
whose writings sowed the seeds of a revolution which enthroned
a prostitute in the Cathedral of Notre Dame. It was at Geneva
that Lenin and Trotsky laid their plans for the Red dawn,
and it was from Geneva that they were transported in sealed
carriages across Germany to destroy Christian Russia, and it
is on the shores of the lake that the Palace of the now defunct
League of Nations stands, a melancholy reminder of an old
truth—'Unless the Lord build the house, they labour in vain
who build it.' There are, of course, no religious symbols in
this temple of secular humanism, and the symbolism of many
of the frescoes is definitely anti-religious. Swinburne's version
of the *Gloria in excelsis*—

Glory to man in the highest

is clearly the theme of the frescoes representing man liberating
himself from the shackles of the past, and it is surely no acci-
dent that Calvin's anti-Rome should today be the one city in

Switzerland in which Communism is strong. No contrast could be greater than that between the spirit of Calvin's Geneva and the spirit of Caux, for the religious war which Calvin waged and the class war which the Communists of Geneva wage are equally alien to the spirit of Caux, where '*les protestants ne protestent plus*'.

Caux is not Mountain House alone. It is a village community consisting of five hotels and smaller pensions. I have tried and failed to find words which can suggest the unique atmosphere of this little world. Superficially there is nothing in their dress or in their manner to differentiate the members of this community from their fellow men, no special habit such as that which separates the monk or friar from the laity, no ritual, no ceremonial to proclaim the essentially religious nature of this society. As I write I remember a young man in a jeep waiting just outside Mountain House to drive somebody down to Montreux. He had a little notebook on his knees. . . . He looked just like any other young man in a jeep or lorry. He might have been a lorry driver noting down some business appointment and not an MRA writing down his guidance. It is this contrast between people who look so ordinary and who are so extraordinary which creates that queer sense of dislocation which is normal in dreamland . . . when people appear in a setting which is not usually theirs.

There is so little at Caux which suggests that an apparently normal cross-section of humanity in point of fact consists of people of whom it is as true as it was of the Israelites of old that 'the Lord hath chosen thee to be his *peculiar people* and to keep all his commandments'.

I remember a dinner at Caux with three 'peculiar people' effectively disguised as accomplished Oxonians, Miss Kirstie Morrison, a graduate and don of my University; Francis Goulding, who speaks eight languages, some of them oriental, and reads fourteen, and who seemed created for the life of a don, and his brother whose urbane and slightly cynical manner suggested anything but an M.R.A. philosophy of life. The talk was, at first, the informed allusive and amusing kind of conversation which one associates with Senior Common rooms. It was only when I raised some point about M.R.A. that the 'peculiar people' emerged from behind the Oxonian façade which they could assume so easily.

Here were three people whose native idiom was the sophisticated idiom of Oxford but who had conquered their dislike of the *simpliste* idiom of Caux. In their case as in many others it is the inner life of M.R.A., not its official presentation, which converted them. The secret of that life is elusive.

> Know you the secret none can utter?

and which none, apparently, can translate into print, for it is notorious that the propaganda of M.R.A. irritates many who would be edified by the inner life of M.R.A. I cannot answer the question, 'Know you the secret?' with a confident affirmative, for I have remained a detached observer, but at least the months which I have spent at Caux have not been wholly wasted. Whatever reserves I may have on the limitations of guidance, I could not doubt but that much will be revealed to those who are sincere in seeking to know the will of God. There is a quality about the Caux way of life which is deeply impressive.

Die Grosse Liebe. An ill-natured comment on an individual is as rare at Caux as a discontented or ill-tempered expression, and there can be few communities catering for over a thousand people where the organisation runs so smoothly and with such a minimum of human friction.

As I bring this book to an end I remember Spengler's melancholy description of the great world cities in which, so he believed, Faith must die. 'The miracle of Cosmopolis, the great petrifact, a symbol of the formless—vast, spreading in its insolence. . . . Here money and intellect celebrate their greatest and their last triumphs.'

But there are other miracles than those of Cosmopolis, and other triumphs than those of 'money and intellect'. Across the portals of Mountain House on the cliffs above Lake Leman might well be inscribed the words which I have placed at the head of this chapter, words which are a challenge and an answer to the pessimism of Spengler.

THUS SAITH PHOCYLIDES, A LITTLE, WELL-ORDERED CITY SET ON A ROCK IS BETTER THAN ALL YOUR FRENZIED NINEVEHS

APPENDIX I

Report of a meeting held to discuss the participation of Catholics in M.R.A. within the diocese of Lausanne, Geneva and Fribourg (Translated from *Orientierung*, 20 (1956), No. 18, p. 204f. the journal of the Institute of Apologetics of the Swiss Catholic Action organization.)

THE following is the substance of a 'gentleman's agreement' reached between some prominent persons in the Church and in M.R.A.:

The participation of Catholics in the team life and in the work of M.R.A. raises problems to the importance of which attention has repeatedly been drawn by ecclesiastical authorities, and in particular by the directions of the Holy Office, dated September 1951 and repeated in March 1955.

In the hope of finding a happy and fruitful solution to these problems the Right Reverend François Charrière, Bishop of Lausanne, Geneva and Fribourg, called together some leading personalities in M.R.A. and a number of priests well acquainted with its work. In the course of this meeting on 8th October 1955, the following eight points were agreed on as the basis for possible co-operation:

1) Christian terminology such as 'the Church', 'the Holy Spirit', 'the Cross of Christ', etc., will be avoided in the official vocabulary of M.R.A.

2) M.R.A. has declared itself to be a 'gateway' to the Church. It will therefore avoid giving the impression that it is a self-sufficient entity, complete in itself. It will not put itself in the place of the Church as regards the giving of religious instruction, but on the contrary it should continue definitely to encourage each of its Catholic members to strengthen their attachment to the Church and to submit to the Church's directions.

3) The object of a Christian's life extends beyond purely temporal aims, even those as noble as 'remaking the world'.

4) 'Quiet times' and 'sharing' can give no absolute certainty

about the will of God. They should therefore never be used as a means of pressure to change a decision or a life commitment. They should always be a humble and sincere seeking after God's will in a spirit of absolute unselfishness.

5) A team will always respect the special vocation of each of its members and will exert no pressure, even indirectly, to influence it in the interests of the work of M.R.A.

6) The Church considers it desirable that Catholics should not come under the moral jurisdiction of non-Catholics. To achieve this purpose Catholic whole-time workers will not be isolated; several of them will always be grouped together. Wherever there are Catholics, their religious instruction shall be ensured through priests in touch with the Bishop of Fribourg. M.R.A. will facilitate such instruction.

7) When participating in a world or continental (European) mission, Catholics will never be used as such for propaganda purposes.

8) The only way to avoid difficulties in Catholic countries is for M.R.A. never to undertake any action in such places without the approval of the local bishop.

After a friendly and frank discussion, Mr. Peter Howard and his friends who attended the meeting accepted the spirit and letter of these propositions, and declared themselves to be ready, in so far as it lay in their power, to see that these eight points were put into effect. After reminding them that he could neither speak for the Catholic Church as a whole, nor prejudge any decision of the Holy Office, Bishop Charrière expressed the definite hope that, if these conditions were exactly followed, the co-operation of Catholics in M.R.A. would develop in an increasingly fruitful way.

APPENDIX II

THE following is a quotation from a chapter in the recently published book, *Aktuelle Moralprobleme* (Patmos-Verlag, Düsseldorf, 1955), by Professor Werner Schöllgen, Dean of the Faculty of Catholic Theology in the University of Bonn, Germany. A translation of the complete chapter can be obtained from M.R.A.. 4 Hays Mews, Berkeley Square, London, W1. Professor Schöllgen is a very distinguished Catholic theologian, and the approval with which he writes of M.R.A. has had a considerable effect in German Catholic circles.

On my second day in Caux I had a talk with a French Professor. I thought an intellectual from Paris must have special difficulty with Moral Re-Armament's allegedly strong American manner of propagation, so I asked him, 'What do you feel about Moral Re-Armament and why have you come here?' He gave me a friendly smile and said, 'I have no theoretical reasons for coming here, but I have had a decisive experience. Just before the war my wife met the Oxford Group (forerunner of Moral Re-Armament) and she brought my grown-up children under its influence. All I can say is that it is only since that time that I have had a happy home life. You must realize that all who are wholly committed to Moral Re-Armament have had an experience of this sort. Moral Re-Armament has changed their lives at crucial points. It is this great experience —the fact that typical modern men and especially those who are no longer reached by the Churches can thus be won to moral and religious ideals—that has led Frank Buchman, even against the opposition of certain sections, to the great re-alignment and transformation of the former Oxford Group into the Moral Re-Armament of today. This has as its purpose the mobilisation of moral forces for the reform of our economy and politics.'

I was especially impressed by conversations fully bearing this out with a number of Asian intellectuals who with one accord said Asia needs a common moral platform as quickly as possible and immediately available. Otherwise Asia will fall victim to Bolshevism in a very few years without war or overt violence.

Such a common platform is certainly not less needed by Europe, which is torn and divided in a thousand different ways. After the first world war Max Scheler in his famous essay 'Peace Between the Religious Confessions'[1] had already called for a rallying of all men of positive ideals in, as it were, concentric circles. After the second world war high Church authorities, and even the highest, spoke in similar vein; and it is highly significant that according to a most reliable report from Rome co-operation with Islam is being demanded.[2]

In Germany as well as elsewhere the familiar arguments of the Integralists have been launched recently against such co-operation. If they are out to make their charges a matter of principle and if they are out to annihilate with the over-sharp weapon of suspicion of heresy any man who differs from them, then their arguments must be strongly countered. It is admittedly quite different if they muster their arguments only on a basis of opportunism, so as to give them a mere tactical importance. Holland and Britain, with their principles of strict ecclesiastical concentration, have managed well. Conditions in Germany are totally different. In the case of the infamous controversy over the trade unions before the first world war, arguments pro and con were lined up in bitter campaigns. Against the existence of Christian trade unions, it was argued that whoever might call in any ethical and religious force to help must embrace the whole Church with all its dogmas and sacraments; otherwise he would be denying the faith indirectly by remaining silent. Today we have a historical perspective wide enough to see how necessary it was to bring all the Christian forces among the workers together on one common platform. In my opinion we in Germany today will not come through without a uniting of all positive forces of whatever nature. Today, Max Scheler is doubly right in his warning against the bald all-or-nothing position. The only winner will be Bolshevism.

And now to the question so frequently posed. Will not some who have been released by Moral Re-Armament from their slavery to Naturalism, and who have been freed from their preoccupation with a purely temporal and superficial world, just stop advancing; and might not even Catholics choose to reduce their religious life to this minimum? My personal impressions, as also many conversations, make me take this question lightly and put it aside with great optimism. *Any man who has once been made aware of ethical and religious elements goes on to seek full truth.*

[1] Scheler, Max, 'Der Friede unter den Konfessionem', in: *Hochland,* 18 (1920-1), 140ff., 464ff.

[2] *Herder-Korrespondenz,* 4 (1950), 156.

Moral Re-Armament is clearly incomplete in three important points. It has no form of worship or institutional framework. Its ethics contain only a teaching of personal attitudes, not principles concerning the objective content of the rules of social life. It puts forward no scientific and systematic confirmation of its ethical content. It is the sheer inner objective reality of these absolutely central elements in the Catholic moral teaching which make it impossible that Moral Re-Armament could ever act as an equal competitor. Its great calling and also its great achievement—this I especially emphasise—seems to me that it speaks to the 'little ones in Christ' and feeds them with 'milk not meat' (1 Cor. 3: 1 f.).

Late one evening I was standing on the empty terrace of the great Caux hotel. Below me, glimmering in the lights, lay Lausanne, at whose University in the first quarter of the century the famous national economist and sociologist, Vilfredo Pareto, had been active. He was the man who gave the world the modern sociological theory of an élite, the idea that the essential factors in history are the small minorities of the so-called leading classes, and that all great changes are actually nothing more than an exchange of élites (*circulations des élites*). Lenin and Mussolini used this theory for their own ends, like a recipe from a cook book. Lenin was then living as an exile in Switzerland; Mussolini was a foreign student in Lausanne. Hitler took over their technique in its broad outlines.

What a deep impression it left upon me that in the open air of the heights above this very university city of Lausanne where Fascism was intellectually formulated men are now meeting to create an élite not of force but of goodwill!

INDEX